Stadium Stories™ Series

D0645989

Stadium Stories:

Oakland Raiders

Colorful Tales of the Silver and Black

Tom LaMarre

The Globe Pequot Press

GUILFORD, CONNECTICUT

Text design: Casey Shain
All photos courtesy of the Oakland Raiders except where noted.

Library of Congress Cataloging-in-Publication Data
LaMarre, Tom.
    Stadium stories : Oakland Raiders / Tom LaMarre.
        p. cm.
    ISBN 0-7627-2737-3
    1. Oakland Raiders (Football team) I. Title.

 GV956.024L36 2003
 796.332'64'0979466–dc21

                                            2003054729

Manufactured in the United States of America
First Edition/First Printing

Contents

Preface

My father took me to my first Raider games at Candlestick Park and Kezar Stadium in San Francisco in 1960 and 1961. In 1964, Sports Editor George Ross of the *Oakland Tribune* hired me when I was a senior at Skyline High in Oakland. With my first paycheck, I bought Raider season tickets.

After leaving the *Tribune* in 1979, I was hired by the *Los Angeles Times*. The Raiders came south in 1982 and I enjoyed watching them in the L.A. Coliseum, but always felt they belonged in Oakland. I was pleased when they returned in 1995.

Naturally, I had to temper my enthusiasm for the Raiders to be an unbiased reporter when I covered the team from 1971–77. But my relationship with the team, while professional in nature, has always been good. Executive assistant Al LoCasale was a valuable resource for me while writing this book. Mike Taylor, Craig Long, and the rest of the public relations staff were of great help.

George Ross and Scotty Stirling, my mentors as a 17-year-old aspiring reporter, were invaluable to me then and now.

I tried to give this story a personal touch. So much so, that I must confess: In the Holy Roller and Holy Toledos chapter, a young fan runs off the field with Clem Daniels—my teacher at Skyline High, my friend, and my all-time favorite Raider.

I was that fan.

In the Beginning

The Oakland Raiders have a penchant for catch phrases, and they like to call their past glory "Decades of Destiny."

The Raiders have played in five Super Bowls, winning three times, and have played in fourteen American Football League or American Football Conference Championship games.

Owner Al Davis and fifteen players who wore the Silver and Black are enshrined in the Pro Football Hall of Fame in Canton, Ohio.

All this from a franchise that was an afterthought when the AFL was formed in 1960, one that was on the verge of folding for much of the first three years, until it began a monumental rise to become one of the finest organizations in sports.

When Davis arrived in Oakland in 1963, more than building a football team, he wanted to create a mystique.

The Chicago Bears, the feared "Monsters of the Midway," were the National Football League champions that year; CBS gave fans a prime-time special, "The Violent World of Sam Huff" in 1962; the Los Angeles Rams had the "Fearsome Foursome"; and Vince Lombardi was a legend in the making, the coach behind the "Green Bay Sweep."

But Davis looked elsewhere for inspiration.

"Growing up in Brooklyn, I had always admired Army, the 'Black Knights of the Hudson,' " Davis said. "They came out in those black jerseys and invoked fear and intimidation. That's what I wanted."

The team that turned around a franchise, the 1963 Oakland Raiders

So the Oakland Raiders' colors of black, gold, and white were almost perfect for Davis, new coach and general manager at the age of thirty-three after serving on Coach Sid Gillman's staff with the Los Angeles Chargers (who moved to San Diego in 1961).

Davis added his own touch and the Silver and Black was born. When the Raiders wore their new uniforms on opening day of the American Football League season at Frank Youell Field, it was love at first sight for Oakland fans.

Coach Hank Stram of the Kansas City Chiefs hated playing the Raiders in Oakland, with imposing Hall of Fame linemen Jim Otto, Art Shell, and Gene Upshaw leading the Raiders onto the field in their black shirts.

These days, there is the raucous "Black Hole" in the south end zone at the Oakland Coliseum; when Shell coached the Raiders, he called their home field "Black Bottom"; and after the Raiders trounced the Washington Redskins in Super Bowl XV, NFL Films called it "Black Sunday."

But uniforms were the least of Davis's worries when he took over in January 1963. The Raiders had stumbled to 2–12 and 1–13 records in the previous two seasons, and even worse, the front office was in shambles.

"It was God-awful," said Scotty Stirling, who was the *Oakland Tribune*'s Raider beat writer at the time and eventually became public relations director and then general manager of the Raiders. "The owners didn't want to spend any money and it was really a skeleton staff. When Al started out, he was doing everything by himself."

Not quite everything. Stirling also would serve as general manager of the Golden State Warriors, then assistant to NBA commissioner Walter Kennedy, and now is scouting director of the Sacramento Kings, but in 1963, while still working for the *Tribune*, he was making travel arrangements for the Raiders.

The Oakland franchise was a poor stepchild from the start, with Minneapolis slated to get the eighth AFL franchise when

the league was founded in 1960. However, the National Football League had coveted Minnesota for several years and made the owners of the new Vikings an offer they could not refuse.

Stirling was working at the *Tribune* in the wee hours one morning in 1959 when he pulled a story off the sports wire that said the AFL was interested in a group in Oakland. Stirling made some phone calls but could find no one who had talked with the AFL.

"It was a fishing expedition by the AFL owners," Stirling said. "Barron Hilton [owner of the Chargers] said he wanted a rival on the West Coast, and if they didn't give him one, he was pulling out.

"The AFL owners hadn't talked to anyone from Oakland, but they thought if they put out a story, they might find some people who were interested."

A group headed by businessmen Wayne Valley, Ed McGah, and Chet Soda was interested and became owners of the AFL's eighth team and members of the self-proclaimed "Foolish Club."

The *Tribune* held a contest for the readers to name the new team. Soda, who also was a city councilman, greeted everyone he met with a hearty "Howdy, Señor!" He rigged the contest and the team was named the Oakland Señors.

In a precursor of the vociferousness for which Oakland fans have become known, there was a tremendous outcry from the community, and the team eventually was called by the name that actually won the contest: Oakland Raiders.

The Raiders, already playing catch-up, had been dealt another blow. While the eighth franchise was in limbo, the other AFL teams raided the roster of the nameless team. Lost were running back Abner Hayes to the Dallas Texans and wide receiver Don Norton to the Chargers, among others.

But the other AFL teams missed the best player of them all, a 200-pound center from University of Miami named Jim Otto, who would become perhaps the best center of all time and a symbol of Raider toughness.

During a game in 1963, Otto was shaken up and took himself out. When he got to the sideline, Davis was waiting for him.

"When I was with the Chargers, we felt if we could get you out of the game, the rest of the team would quit because you are the leader of this team," Davis said.

Otto never again left the field under his own power when the Raiders had the ball.

Despite nine knee surgeries, Otto never missed a start in his fifteen-year career, playing 210 consecutive games between 1960 and 1974 to begin a tradition of Raider durability at center. Only Dave Dalby, Don Mosebar, and Barret Robbins have followed him as regular starters at the position in the team's long history.

"What Al said to me became etched indelibly in my mind," Otto said. "I took a beating sometimes, but I stayed in the game. I didn't want to disappoint him, the fans, my family, or my teammates. I was the captain for twelve or thirteen years and I guess I was a leader.

Center Jim Otto never missed a regular-season game in his Raider career.

"It was hard sometimes, especially because I had a chronic problem with my neck. I would get a stinger and it would just about knock me out. But there was no way I was going to come out of the game. What he said that one time was enough."

Coach Eddie Erdelatz, who first saw Otto when his Navy team played Miami, laid the cornerstone for the Raider franchise when he put Otto at center in 1960.

The Raiders also found quarterback Tom Flores and guard Wayne Hawkins, who had played just over an hour away at College of the Pacific in Stockton, and they helped Oakland post a respectable 6–8 record that first season.

But the next two years were disastrous, and Erdelatz gave way to Red Conkright and then Marty Feldman. (Not bug-eyed Marty Feldman the comedian, but that would have been fitting.)

The Raiders were 3–25 the next two seasons, losing nineteen consecutive games until a 20–0 victory over the Boston Patriots in the last game of the 1962 season, before a crowd generously listed at 8,000.

"There will be dancing on Broadway tonight," said Raider radio announcer Bob Blum as the final seconds of that game ticked away, but it had to be a joke because almost nobody in Oakland or the East Bay cared.

The Raiders played at Kezar Stadium and Candlestick Park in San Francisco their first two seasons before the city of Oakland made the first vital move to establishing a home for the team. Frank Youell Field, which was named after an undertaker and held about 22,000 spectators, was built at Exposition Field—where Oakland youngsters had played Young America baseball for decades.

Paul Maguire, who played for the Chargers and the Buffalo Bills, called the stadium motif "early erector set." The stadium was a joke in many quarters, but it gave the Raiders a place to play in Oakland until the 53,000-seat Oakland Coliseum was finished in 1966.

But even the construction of a new stadium didn't stop rumors and reports that the Raiders were headed elsewhere. Throughout their first five years, there were stories that the team would be moving to Sacramento, Portland, Seattle, Salt Lake City, Reno, or Las Vegas.

"Most of those stories came out of San Francisco, appearing in the *Chronicle* or the *Examiner*," said George Ross, who was sports editor of the *Oakland Tribune*. "When a story would appear in the paper, we would have to track down Wayne Valley or Joe Foss [AFL commissioner] to knock the story down.

"When Al Davis came to Oakland, he stopped talking to the San Francisco press for a while. He realized he didn't need them anyway because there weren't many Raider fans in San Francisco, which had the 49ers. Al knew it was more important for him to reach the fans in Contra Costa County and Southern Alameda County, whom he would need to fill the Coliseum when it opened."

Valley, who would later lose control of the Raiders because of it, changed everything with one masterstroke when he hired Davis.

"I had a dream, to build the finest organization in sports," Davis said.

Slogans that Davis posted around the Raiders' offices that first year, "Pride and Poise," "Commitment to Excellence," and "Pro Football's Dynamic Organization" are still bywords in Oakland.

One of the first things Davis did was send the Raiders out into the community, not only in Oakland, but into the entire East Bay area and as far away as Sacramento.

Al Davis

E ven though he wasn't there when the team was founded in 1960,
Al Davis is the Oakland Raiders. The Raiders' fortunes turned
instantly when Wayne Valley, one of the team's original owners,
lured assistant coach Davis from the San Diego Chargers in 1963 to be
coach and general manager in Oakland.

"If I said Al Davis was lovable, I'd be a liar," Valley once said. "You
don't have to love him, just turn him loose."

Valley turned Davis loose and the result has been one of the most
remarkable chapters in sports history.

A successful contractor and businessman, Valley was smart enough
to know he needed Davis to make the Raiders a success and that the
day would come when they would battle for control of the team. Valley's
mistake was underestimating Davis, figuring he could outmaneuver a
football coach.

Davis coached only three seasons and the Raiders' record under
him was 23–16–3, unremarkable until stacked against the 9–33 of
their first three seasons.

"He was one of the great coaches I have ever observed. . . a truly
great coach," said Bill Walsh, a former Raider assistant who created
the San Francisco 49ers' dynasty. "Had he chosen to remain in coaching, he would be considered one of the great coaches of all time."

American Football League team owners were fighting the "Pro
Football War" with the established National Football League in 1966
and knew they needed their most ruthless commander to overcome the
established league.

Davis, who would never coach again, went to New York and became
AFL commissioner. His ingenious plan to sign the NFL's quarterbacks,
some to future contracts that would take effect when their current
deals expired, helped force a merger within eight weeks.

Returning to Oakland as managing general partner of the Raiders,
Davis gained one-third of the controlling interest in the team. Valley
and Ed McGah Sr. each had the other thirds.

*Al Davis receives the Vince Lombardi Trophy
from his archrival, Pete Rozelle.*

Valley returned from a European vacation in the early 1970s to learn Davis and McGah had signed a contract giving Davis controlling interest in the team. The contract held up in court and Davis had control of the Raiders.

The Raiders are Davis's life. The only time he was not on the job was when his wife, Carol, was in a coma in an Oakland hospital in 1979. Davis was at her bedside, virtually twenty-four hours a day, until she awoke several weeks later.

When the Raiders' lease in Oakland was up and an agreement to stay was taken off the table, Davis moved the team to Los Angeles in 1982. When the lease at the Los Angeles Coliseum ran its course and promises to Davis were not kept, he moved the Raiders back to Oakland in 1995.

Davis and the Raiders have endured numerous lawsuits along the way, but their record in court is as impressive as it is on the field.

"That first winter, he had us out meeting people and promoting the team," Otto recalled. "We hadn't done too much of that in the first three years. I thought it was just to sell tickets, but it was more than that. We were creating a relationship with the fans. It was great for us and for them."

A love affair developed between the fans and the Raiders, who partied with their supporters in the parking lot after games at Frank Youell Field and later at the Coliseum and in bars all over the East Bay.

After wearing several hats in his first year in Oakland, Davis eventually made three key front-office hirings that stabilized the franchise, making Stirling public relations director, Ron Wolf director of scouting, and Al LoCasale his executive assistant.

All three had specific areas of expertise but also would be valuable lieutenants for Davis and the AFL during the "Pro Football War" with the NFL.

"I knew I would end up working for the Raiders," Stirling said. "But Al [Davis] told me he needed me more writing for the *Tribune* at first."

LoCasale handled, among many other chores, the day-to-day operation of the franchise, allowing Davis to concentrate on football.

Wolf, who had been working for *Pro Football Illustrated*, was a former intelligence officer in the U.S. Army who was stationed at Checkpoint Charlie in West Berlin during the Cold War.

Davis had brought the Chargers' front-office system with him to Oakland, a system that Gillman had copied from his days with the Los Angeles Rams. Wolf and LoCasale refined it to fit the Raiders' needs.

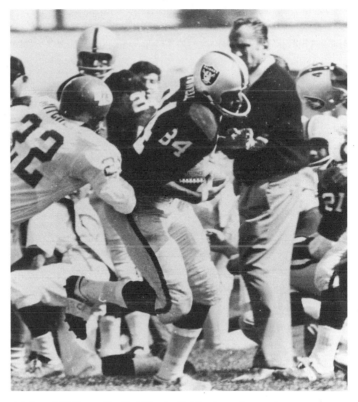

Art Powell (84) was the first big signing by general manager and coach Al Davis.

Wolf built the Raiders' scouting system, which is pretty much the same now as it was then. The Raiders are one of the few teams in the NFL who do all of their own scouting, rather than joining with other teams in scouting "combines" to share information.

One of Wolf's first moves when he was appointed general manager of the Green Bay Packers in 1991 was acquiring unknown quarterback Brett Favre from the Atlanta Falcons, paving the way for the Pack's return to greatness, a move similar to the first bold stroke by Davis when he came to the Raiders in 1963.

Davis had gained great insight into both sides of the passing game under Gillman in San Diego. On defense, he wanted defensive linemen who could rush the passer and cornerbacks who could cover wide receivers man to man. On offense, he wanted huge linemen to pass block, a strong-armed quarterback, and big, swift wide receivers.

So he set out to acquire them by signing wide receiver Art Powell, 6'3" and 210 pounds, a veteran of the Canadian Football League, who had played out his option with the New York Titans (later the Jets) and was one of football's first free agents.

"Al was really excited about Powell, more than I was at first," Flores said. "I knew he was good, but I had no idea how good until we started working together. Art had that combination of size and speed that you don't see very often, and he had great hands. He would have been a great player in any era.

"That was the first player Al signed for the Raiders, but it was a preview of what was to come. He knew what kind of players he wanted and the type of players we had to have to get better. So he went out and got them."

Davis shocked the Raiders, and Flores in particular, by cutting tackle Jack Stone and guard Charlie Brown, both starters, after the final exhibition game.

The Raiders signed Frank Youso, who was cut by the Minnesota Vikings because he didn't get along with Coach Norm Van Brocklin, and elevated reserve Proverb Jacobs to the other starting tackle spot. To round out the line with Otto and Hawkins, Davis acquired tough but undersized guard Sonny Bishop from the Houston Oilers.

"I was nervous going into the season behind guys I didn't know," Flores said. "But we won the first two games and I realized those were very good moves. We had better players in those positions.

"In the first year of the AFL, all the teams were pretty close in talent. But the Dallas Texans and the Chargers had gone to a higher level. Al had been with the Chargers and he understood what we had to do to reach that level."

There are people who believe the 1963 Chargers were the best team in football, especially on offense. They had tackle Ron Mix and wide receiver Lance Alworth, both members of the Pro Football Hall of Fame.

San Diego had exceptional quarterbacks Tobin Rote and John Hadl, and explosive runners Paul Lowe and Keith Lincoln. On defense, they had linebackers Maguire and Frank Buncom and defensive tackle Earl Faison. And the Chargers also had many lesser-known but solid players throughout a roster that Davis had helped Gillman put together.

"I've never seen anyone who understood talent better than [Davis] did," Stirling said. "Sure, he made mistakes, everybody does in evaluating talent. But by and large he was almost infallible when it came to making personnel decisions. Just in those first few years, look at the players he brought in from other teams. Powell was only the first one. After that, we got Billy Cannon, Willie Brown, George Blanda, Daryle Lamonica, Hewritt Dixon, and more. People thought some of them were washed up, but he got great football out of all of them."

Davis also took advantage of another castoff, running back Clem Daniels, who had been a defensive back with the Texans before coming to the Raiders late in 1961. Oakland switched him to running back and he rushed for 766 yards and seven touchdowns on a pitiful team in 1962.

But Davis, who had been called "a young genius" by editor Herman Masin of *Scholastic Coach* magazine, saw something else in the 6', 215-pound Daniels. Even in the "Airborne Football League," what Davis did with his running back was revolutionary, sending Daniels deep down the field on pass routes reserved for wide receivers. He was chased by linebackers who could not keep up.

"Clem was a power runner but he also was very fast and had great hands," Flores said. "Linebackers just could not stay with him. We utilized all the abilities he had. The next back the Raiders had who could do all those things well, and maybe a little better, was Marcus Allen. But Clem was a great player who was ahead of his time.

"I didn't know we were going to be as good a team as we turned out to be, but I knew in my first meeting with Al that we were going to be better. He was showing me things that we were going to do on the blackboard and pretty soon I started smiling. It was a quarterback's dream.

"Al looked at me and asked, 'What's wrong?' I told him, 'Nothing. This is going to be fun.' "

It was fun for the Raiders and their fans in 1963, except for a four-game losing streak, when Daniels was slowed by a deep thigh bruise. But the Raiders rebounded by winning their last eight games, including their first two victories ever over the hated Chargers.

Daniels, the AFL's most valuable player that season, rushed for 1,099 yards and caught thirty passes for 685 yards, a 22.8 average, and five touchdowns.

Powell, who is still prominent in the Raider record book despite the likes of Fred Biletnikoff, Cliff Branch, Warren Wells, Tim Brown, Jerry Rice, and others who followed, caught seventy-three passes for 1,304 yards and sixteen touchdowns.

Flores and Cotton Davidson alternated at quarterback and opponents could not stop Oakland's famed East, or slot, formation.

Davis would line up Powell in the "slot" inside either Bo Roberson or Dobie Craig, both fleet receivers, to create a mismatch for Powell against a safety. If the defense moved the off-side cornerback over to cover Powell, it opened up the backside for Daniels.

"I think we were the first team to really develop the slot formation, which we call East," Flores said. "I loved that formation, as a player and a coach. We would create mismatches for Art or Clem against a safety or linebacker and then send them deep. I could throw the ball far enough; all I had to do was wait for the play to develop. I remember Al yelling at me so many times to hold the ball longer."

Davis didn't have nearly as much on the other side of the ball other than defensive end Dan Birdwell, who would make a name for himself with Oakland's "Eleven Angry Men" in 1967 after moving to tackle, and cornerback Fred "The Hammer" Williamson. But Davis picked up savvy middle linebacker Archie Matsos from Buffalo and outfoxed opponents by changing defenses almost every week.

"We would go into the locker room after the game and opposing coaches were complaining almost every week that the game films they had of the Raiders were almost useless," said George Ross, the *Tribune* sports editor.

"Davis gave Matsos the freedom to freelance and he was making plays all over the field. Then the Raiders had some headhunters in the secondary so receivers were always looking around when they ran their pass routes. It was all very effective."

Oakland defeated San Diego for the first time, 34–33, on Davidson's 10-yard touchdown pass to fullback Glenn Shaw with 1:52 left at Balboa Stadium on October 27, but the rematch on December 7 at Frank Youell Field was even better and the beginning of another Raider tradition.

The Raiders are known for their remarkable comebacks—and this was the first one.

San Diego built a 27–10 lead after three quarters and a light rain began to fall. Youell Field had been full, but the fans started to leave and soon the stadium was nearly half empty. But the Raiders were on the move.

Oakland forced four turnovers in the final quarter, and Davidson threw two touchdown passes and ran for another on a quarterback draw as the Raiders scored thirty-one points, still a team record for one quarter, to post an improbable 41–27 victory.

After their last touchdown with 1:06 remaining, Davis had the audacity to try an onside kick, and Shaw recovered.

Most of the fans who left returned. Some who were driving away tuned into the game on their car radios and heard the rally begin. Frank Youell Field was nearly filled when the game ended.

"That was incredible, especially because it was against the Chargers," Otto said. "We proved something to ourselves and to our fans that day, to never accept anything but victory."

LoCasale, who was still with San Diego at the time, added, "We knew when Al went to Oakland that things were going to change, but not necessarily that quickly. We used to tell players to shape up or we would send them to Oakland. Those days were over.

"I remember one day we were working on the draft and we took a little break. [Assistant coach] Joe Madro said, 'Do you think Al is taking a break up in Oakland?' So we went back to work."

The Raiders finished with a 10–4 record and one of the best one-season turnarounds in pro football history. With another incredible victory, 52–49, over the Houston Oilers in the season finale, they wound up one game behind the Chargers in the AFL's Western Division.

Flores, who had missed the 1962 season because he had tuberculosis, showed he was back at full strength by throwing six touchdown passes, and George Blanda of the Oilers, four years before coming to the Raiders, threw five.

"The score was tied, 35–35, at halftime, and it was so narrow leaving the field at Frank Youell you had to walk right next to guys on the other team," Flores recalled. "I was walking next to George, who could be an ornery guy, and he was cussing, 'Thirty-five points and we're tied.'

"That was a great way to finish what was a miracle season for us. We finished behind the Chargers, so that game was like the playoffs for us."

Powell, Daniels, Otto, Matsos, and Williamson were selected to the All-AFL team, and Davis was chosen AFL Coach of the Year and the city of Oakland's Young Man of the Year.

The second half of Wayne Valley's prophecy had come true.

"I knew when I hired Al Davis that it would eventually come down to him and me for control of the team," Valley would say later. "But I also knew he was the man we needed to make the Raiders successful."

The first half would come later when Davis would take total control of the Raiders.

Grand Old Man

E ven among the legends in the Pro Football Hall of Fame, George Blanda is unique.

Fans can compare Joe Montana with John Elway, Johnny Unitas, and Bart Starr.

For Jim Brown, there are O. J. Simpson, Gale Sayers and Walter Payton.

For Bronko Nagurski, there are Ernie Nevers, Red Grange, and Jim Thorpe.

But no one in National Football League history had a career to compare with the twenty-six-year saga of Blanda, a quarterback and kicker who also played linebacker and defensive back in his first few seasons in the league.

In fact you can argue that Blanda actually had three careers after leaving the University of Kentucky as a ninth-round draft choice of the Chicago Bears in 1949.

Blanda was mostly a backup quarterback for the Bears in nine seasons before a contract squabble with coach and owner George Halas, one of the NFL's founders, left Blanda out of football in 1959.

But the American Football League opened shop in 1960, and Blanda was one of its first stars with the Houston Oilers, leading them to the first two AFL championships.

Cut loose by the Oilers at the age of forty in 1967, Blanda became a folk hero in nine seasons with the Oakland Raiders, helping them reach Super Bowl II in his first season and nearly carrying them on his back to another in his miracle season of 1970.

"I did have three careers," Blanda said. "I was fortunate after the first two that there was someone else who wanted to pick me up. With the AFL starting in 1960, it was especially good timing for me. I enjoyed my time with all three teams, and they were all different. I was the darling of the fans in Chicago because they always love the backup quarterback. In Houston I was playing quarterback and kicking, and we were winning in the first few years. In Oakland I was like a relief pitcher, and if the starter got hurt or into trouble, they would bring me in."

All of this after his college coach, the legendary Paul "Bear" Bryant, told Halas that Blanda, whose twenty-six years and 340 games are NFL records, would never make it in pro football.

Bryant wasn't the only one who held that opinion when Blanda joined the Bears, who already had heralded quarterbacks Sid Luckman, Johnny Lujack, and Bobby Layne.

"George Blanda was not a very good football player when he came to the Chicago Bears," Lujack said. "He was rusty in the fine points of T-formation quarterback, but he was a determined young player.

"They tried to play him at linebacker, but he was no linebacker. He couldn't run the ball at all, so they had to find a use for his talents. But I believe he might have been the finest kicker of the football I have ever seen."

His strong right leg gave Blanda a spot on the roster, so he went about polishing his other skills and made the most of his opportunities. In his first exhibition game with the Bears, Blanda threw a 40-yard touchdown pass to George McAfee on his first play and completed all seven of his passes, three for touchdowns.

"There were no guaranteed contracts or multiyear deals in those days," Blanda recalled. "You had a one-year contract, and

Reclamation Projects

The Raiders have a history of taking players who had problems elsewhere or were considered washed up or too old and getting great football from them.

George Blanda was too old, John Matuszak and Bob Brown were too much trouble, and Jerry Rice and Ronnie Lott were past their primes, but all delivered when they came to the Raiders.

"We don't judge people by what happened when they were somewhere else," Coach John Madden once said. "We judge them by what happens when they come here."

Jim Plunkett came off the scrap heap and led the Raiders to two Super Bowl victories.

Jim Plunkett had lost it, but after being out of football, he quarterbacked the Raiders to two Super Bowl victories.

Rich Gannon was a career backup before setting passing records for the Raiders and leading them to Super Bowl XXXVII.

There have been dozens of others, including Eric Dickerson, Bubba Smith, Rod Woodson, Lyle Alzado, Roger Craig, Billy Cannon, Cedrick Hardman, Bill Romanowski, James Lofton, Zack Crockett, Tom Rathman, Greg Pruitt, Burgess Owens, and Vince Evans.

Great names who gave the Raiders some great football when others thought they had none left to give.

Many felt like Lott, who said: "In my heart, I always felt like a Raider."

you had to produce or you could be cut at any time. It meant every game could be your last. Actually, it was good for me those first few years because I sat on the bench and learned the game and gained experience for when I got the chance to play. I didn't get beat up and that helped me later on, because when I went to Houston, I was healthy."

Layne, Lujack, and Luckman were gone in a few years, and Blanda spent the rest of his time in Chicago battling the likes of Ed Brown, Bobby Williams, Zeke Bratkowski, and Rudy Bukich for the starting job.

Blanda was the starter in 1953 and 1954, throwing twenty-nine touchdown passes, but he suffered a shoulder separation and lost his job. He was a reserve quarterback after that until "Papa Bear" Halas wanted Blanda to take a cut in pay and be solely a kicker in 1959.

"Halas was a great coach but the only problem I had with him, the problem all the players had with him, was that we didn't get paid very much," Blanda said. "That was the only area of disagreement I ever had with him. We had several other quarterbacks in 1959 and I knew I was gone."

But Blanda was not washed up, and he proved it when the AFL came along.

He joined a Houston team that also had wide receiver Charley Hennigan and running back Billy Cannon, a future teammate with the Raiders, and helped the AFL change the face of football with a wide-open passing game.

"It was a great group of guys and a great team with a lot of speed," Blanda said. "It was exciting to start something new and I was proud of playing in the AFL. I felt, even in the early years, that we had some teams that were as good as a lot of teams in the other league.

"We had to do things to get the fans and the television people interested, so we threw the ball. I threw the ball 68 times in one game, 58 in another, 55, 50. It was a fun period of time."

Blanda and the Oilers won their first game, 37–22, over the Raiders at Kezar Stadium in San Francisco and won the 1960 AFL Championship with a 24–16 victory over the Los Angeles Chargers at Jeppesen Stadium in Houston, with Blanda passing for 301 yards.

In 1962 Blanda passed for 464 yards in one game and seven touchdowns in another as the Oilers won their last ten games, including a 13–6 victory over the Chargers at Balboa Stadium in the AFL title game in San Diego, where the Chargers had relocated in their second season.

Blanda threw thirty-six touchdown passes that season and was the AFL's most valuable player.

The Oilers were in the championship game again in 1962, but they lost to the Dallas Texans (who would become the Kansas City Chiefs), 20–17, on a field goal by Tommy Brooker in the second overtime.

"We should have won three championships, but I made some bad plays in that game and we lost," Blanda recalled. "It was a little ironic because I went to Kansas City to see the Raiders play in 2002, and they were honoring the Texans' team that beat us in 1962. I felt a little responsible for that."

The Oilers were competitive in the next few years but things began to unravel. The "Pro Football War" was raging between the AFL and NFL, and the competition to sign the best players coming out of college was fierce.

Houston did not keep pace.

"We had some great drafts but our owner, Bud Adams, wasn't willing to pay enough money to sign the top young players," Blanda said. "We drafted players like Mike Ditka, Tommy Nobis, and Charley Taylor, but we couldn't sign any of them. Our team got older, and we didn't do anything to upgrade and we didn't improve."

In 1967 Blanda was again out of a job and seemingly finished when the Oilers placed him on waivers, but he got a phone call from Al Davis and the most amazing chapter of his career was about to begin.

The Raiders were building a Super Bowl team and Davis was adding Blanda, cornerback Willie Brown, quarterback Daryle Lamonica, and rookie guard Gene Upshaw as the final pieces to the puzzle. Upshaw and Brown would later join Blanda in the Hall of Fame.

"Those last nine years that meant so much to me would not have happened had [Davis] not been willing to give me a chance," Blanda said. "Playing for the Raiders was a thrill. It was a tough, hard-nosed team, like the Bears.

George Blanda gets off a pass with a timely block from Gene Upshaw.

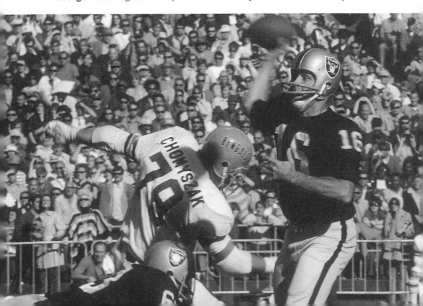

"I was forty years old when I went to play for the Raiders, and we had a lot of new players coming in at the same time. We had great chemistry and started winning immediately. We started a great tradition there in Oakland."

Blanda's role as Lamonica's backup was well defined, and he threw only thirty-eight passes that first season in Oakland, hardly a warm-up compared with his days in Houston, but he led the league with 116 points by kicking twenty field goals and missing only one of fifty-seven extra points.

And the wily veteran served another key role during his time with the Raiders by taking young players such as Warren Wells, Raymond Chester, and Kenny "Snake" Stabler under his wing and preparing them for the rigors of the NFL.

Off the football field, however, Blanda showed no respect for the young guys.

"I remember the first time Mike Siani and Phil Villapiano played golf with Blanda," said Upshaw, one of the Raiders' captains. "They were young guys right out of college, and they thought he was just some old guy. He took all their money that day."

Blanda worked extensively with Wells and Chester on the practice field and developed a feel for what the young players were capable of that would pay off when the old man was called on to perform his miracles in 1970.

But perhaps his most vital contribution to the Raiders was counseling Stabler, always something of a rebel, when he came out of Alabama in 1968. Blanda helped mold him into the quarterback who would lead the Raiders throughout most of their glory days in the 1970s.

"We had a natural bond for a couple of reasons," Stabler said. "We both played for Coach Bryant in college, and we were both quarterbacks with pretty much the same philosophy about the game. He definitely grabbed me and gave me the advice I needed when I came to the Raiders.

"George talked to me and was always there for me. Daryle was the starter, so George and I would spend a lot of time on the sideline or behind the huddle in practice. He did most of the talking and I did most of the listening. They were good lessons I learned.

"I wanted to play right away, but George, who had been through the same thing in Chicago, told me to take my time, keep my eyes and ears open, and learn the game. He was right."

Nonetheless, the impetuous Stabler spoke out about not playing and asked to be traded. Davis and Coach John Madden knew what they had and weren't about to let Stabler go.

Once, when Stabler asked to be traded, Davis actually told him, "Go stand on your head."

"Kenny and I got along very well," Blanda said. "He was anxious to play like most young players, but I told him to be patient and learn for a few years. A lot of young quarterbacks are ruined if they are thrown in there right away.

"He wanted to be traded, but I told him he would be better off staying with a great team like the Raiders rather than going to a team that wasn't so good. He might get a chance to play right away, but he might get beat up, too. Kenny listened and he was ready when he got his chance."

Veterans also learned Blanda was paying attention even when he was standing on the sidelines watching.

Blanda came into a game against Kansas City and called a running play that Upshaw, an All-Pro guard on his way to the Hall of Fame, thought was doomed to failure. He told Blanda in the huddle, but it didn't matter.

"He said to run the play anyway," Upshaw said. "I had to

pull and block a guy on the other side of the field, but I didn't think I could get there in time to make the block because of where he was lined up. So we ran the play and darned if we didn't score a touchdown.

"I asked George how he knew it would work, and he said he had noticed a few plays before that the guy I had to block had moved a bit closer, just enough for me to be able to make the block. He really understood the game."

Wells also benefited from Blanda's wealth of experience.

Davis had discovered the fleet young receiver from Texas Southern. While watching film of a Kansas City game one day, he thought he was seeing things. It appeared that Otis Taylor, the Chiefs' brilliant receiver, was on both sides of the field at the same time.

It was Wells, doing a great imitation of Taylor, only faster. When the Chiefs tried to sneak Wells through waivers, Davis claimed him.

When Wells came to the Raiders and started working with the second team, Blanda was the backup quarterback, and he worked for hours with the young talent, showing the Raiders exactly what they had.

With Lamonica throwing touchdown passes, the Raiders would build big leads before Blanda and Wells would come in for Act II and more of the same.

"Almost every time, I would come in and throw the bomb to Warren," Blanda said. "He would get open and catch everything you threw to him. He could really run the corner and the post, and he would catch the ball no matter where you threw it."

Wells became the perfect complement to Fred Biletnikoff, who ran perhaps the most precise patterns of any receiver in history. Wells caught forty-two touchdown passes in three and a half seasons before going to prison in 1971 for violating the terms of his probation on a gun charge. When he got out of prison two years later, the magic was gone. He couldn't even make the team.

Blanda always made it "Showtime" when he came in to mop up at the end of games, and the Raiders' fans would stick around to watch.

"We didn't believe in running out the clock," Blanda said. "We weren't trying to run up the score, but when you are sitting on the bench and you get a chance to play, you want to show what you can do.

"One time, we were playing against Cincinnati and Paul Brown was their coach. I always had a lot of respect for him, but I had never played for a team that beat him when he was coaching in Cleveland and I was with the Bears. We were beating the Bengals pretty good and we got to the 1 yard line with time running out. Instead of letting the game end, I called a play and we scored a touchdown.

"Paul Brown was just beside himself. I got a little satisfaction from that."

The competitor in Blanda just couldn't walk away.

He showed it again in his only start of his career for the Raiders, when Lamonica suffered back spasms before the game, throwing four touchdown passes in a 43–7 victory at Denver in 1968. The Raiders had a 12–0 lead on every type of scoring play—a touchdown, extra point, safety, and field goal—before the Broncos ran an offensive play. Blanda never let up all day.

"George was the most competitive person I've ever known, and I've been around a lot of competitive guys," Stabler said. "He was good at everything he ever tried. He was a scratch golfer, he played pool and basketball, and he wanted to win. He wanted to beat you.

"Because I wanted to hang around with him and learn

everything I could, we would play 'gin' on road trips. I'd give him my $25 or $50, whatever it was, on every trip. In about my fourth year, I had one of those no-brainer hands and I beat him for the first time.

"He was so mad, he threw the cards on the floor and wouldn't speak to me. He wouldn't even sit next to me on the plane because I beat him once in four years."

Stabler got to see many of Blanda's exploits up close because he was the holder on extra points and field goals.

Although many people were stunned by the things Blanda was doing in his forties, Stabler said, "I was never surprised because I was around him all the time and knew what he could do. Maybe if it had been someone else, but George never surprised me."

Blanda proved any doubters wrong in 1970.

"We got off to a slow start that year and I don't know why," Blanda said. "We had the same players as the last few years and had added some people, so we should have been better. We were struggling a bit and then Daryle got hurt.

"I was just in the right place at the right time. But I've never said I did all those things by myself. We had a great team and we did them together. I couldn't have done anything without a great line and receivers. It was a team thing."

The Raiders, who had won three consecutive division titles, were 2–2–1 on October 25, when Lamonica went down with an injury against the Pittsburgh Steelers in a game at the Oakland Coliseum.

Stabler was the quarterback of the future, but Madden didn't hesitate, sending Blanda into the game with the score tied, 7–7, in the second quarter.

"There was never any question," Stabler said. "I knew George was the next one up. He had been in that situation so many times before. He had been in every situation before."

Blanda came in and threw three touchdown passes to Raymond Chester, and the Raiders came away with a 31–14 victory. Blanda made headlines, but no one had any idea what was coming.

The following week in Kansas City against the hated Chiefs, Oakland was trailing, 17–14, in the closing minutes when quarterback Len Dawson of the Chiefs ran a bootleg for a first down that seemed to seal the Raiders' fate.

But a surreal chain of events led to an improbable finish.

After Dawson picked up the necessary yardage for the first down, he hit the ground. Defensive end Ben Davidson, trailing the play, plowed into Dawson and was flagged for a personal foul and a melee ensued. Both benches emptied as Otis Taylor grabbed Davidson and also was called for a personal foul.

"Dawson was on the ground, but he hadn't been touched down yet," the 6'8" Davidson said innocently later. "I was just making sure he stayed down."

When officials sorted things out, Dawson's run was nullified by offsetting penalties; the Chiefs failed to pick up the first down on their second try and were forced to punt. Lamonica's passes to Biletnikoff moved the Raiders into position for a 48-yard field-goal attempt by Blanda.

Coach Hank Stram of the Chiefs added a little more drama by deploying 6'9" tight end Morris Stroud under the goal post to try to knock the kick away, but the ball cleared Stroud's fingertips and the crossbar in the gathering darkness at Memorial Stadium.

"I had never seen that done before," Blanda said of Stram's ploy. "But there haven't been that many 6'9" football players. The Chargers had Ernie Ladd, but he weighed 300 pounds and couldn't jump like Stroud. The ball cleared Stroud's hand by about 3 feet.

"Daryle got us into position, and John looked at me and said to go kick it. You don't think of what can go wrong in that situation. I would just go through the basics: don't get too fast, keep your head down, and get your steps right. You can't think about missing."

The following week, the Raiders trailed Cleveland, 20–13, in the closing minutes at Oakland. Madden, looking for some more magic, replaced Lamonica with Blanda, who drove the Raiders toward the tying touchdown.

The Raiders reached the Cleveland 14 yard line and called time out.

"George came over to the sideline and we were talking about which play to call," Madden said. "George said if I would let him call three straight posts to Warren Wells, he would guarantee one of them would be a touchdown. I told him to go do it."

On first down Blanda threw incomplete for Wells, but on second down he threw a low fastball that Wells cradled for a touchdown. Blanda added the extra point to tie the score with 1:14 left on the clock.

After the Raiders kicked off, Cleveland tried to get into position for a winning field goal rather than settle for a tie, but Bill Nelsen's pass was intercepted by cornerback Kent McCloughan.

The Raiders were out of field-goal range, but Blanda threw a swing pass to fullback Hewritt Dixon, who ran to the Cleveland 45, and the Raiders called another time-out with seven seconds remaining.

"I went to the sideline and John asked me what I thought," Blanda said. "What I thought was that I was tired. I was forty-three-years-old and had been in for fourteen or fifteen consecutive plays and I was bushed. I told John I didn't think I could throw the ball 50 yards, but I might be able to kick it that far."

Blanda was deadly on kicks of 40 yards and in, but at that point in his career, the Raiders rarely tried kicks of more than 45 yards because his range was dwindling. In fact the 48-yarder in Kansas City was his longest as a Raider to that point, although he made a 55-yarder for Houston earlier in his career.

But this was a magical season.

"I was down on the sidelines, and George had such an air of confidence about him that I really thought he had a chance to make it," Raider executive Al LoCasale said. "When he went back onto the field after the time-out, it was like he was going out to kick an extra point."

Even though it was officially ruled a 52-yard field goal, the film shows the ball was a shade under 53 yards away when Stabler placed it on the ground. The Browns also had a player under the crossbar, but the kick would have been good from at least 55 yards.

Blanda was mobbed by his teammates, and Bill King, on Raider radio, proclaimed: "George Blanda has just been elected king of the world."

By now, even though ESPN and CNN did not yet exist, Blanda was receiving national acclaim thanks to syndicated columnists from Jim Murray to Erma Bombeck, and Howard Cosell's halftime highlights on ABC's *Monday Night Football*.

Radio stations in the Bay Area were caught up in Blanda Fever, and the slogan, "Let George Do It," was being printed on T-shirts, placards, and buttons.

In Denver on week four of Blanda's run, the Raiders were again trailing, 19–17, when Blanda got the call with four minutes remaining, and he led an 80-yard touchdown drive.

Blanda hit Fred Biletnikoff, who ran a flawless corner pattern, for the game-winning touchdown that covered 20 yards in the final minute.

"That one was pretty easy because Freddie could get open against anybody," Blanda said. "Denver blitzed me, and I always liked that because I had a quick release and they seldom got to me. If you get the ball to the right guy against the blitz, you can make a big play.

George Blanda's field goal gives the Raiders a victory over San Diego in 1970.

"When we got to the 30, we would always start going for the end zone because it's easier to score from there on a pass play than when you get closer. When they blitzed, my first instinct was Freddie to the corner and, as usual, he was open."

The final game of Blanda's amazing streak was not as dramatic, other than the fact that there were only four seconds left when he kicked a 16-yard field goal (the posts were on the goal line in those days rather than on the end line) to lift the Raiders to a 20–17 victory over San Diego.

Blanda doesn't take much credit for that one.

"I didn't do very much," he said. "Daryle did a great job of getting us into position for a chip shot. All I had to do was keep my head down and kick it."

Blanda's heroics helped the Raiders win the AFC West title with an 8–4–2 record, and he would play a role in another remarkable victory on December 6 in New York. After Lamonica threw a 33-yard touchdown pass to Wells with one second left, Blanda kicked the extra point to beat the Jets, 14–13.

Even though he was a part-time player who threw only fifty-five passes that season, Blanda was selected AFC Player of the Year and NFL Man of Year.

When Blanda was inducted into the Hall of Fame in 1981, Al Davis made the presentation.

"It would be accurate to say that his miracle season in 1970 made the greatest impact for heroism and thrills that the game has ever known," Davis said.

Even in Canton, that's indisputable.

Becoming
a Superpower

After Al Davis helped create the Super Bowl, his next goal was to create a Super Bowl team.

Davis left his coaching post with the Oakland Raiders in April 1966 to become commissioner of the American Football League during the "Pro Football War." Davis's brilliant plan to sign the National Football League's top quarterbacks forced the established league to seek terms for a merger only eight weeks later.

The merger created the Super Bowl, and Davis returned to the Raiders as managing general partner to build a team in Oakland that could play in football's biggest game.

In 1966 the Raiders finished second to the Kansas City Chiefs in the AFL's Western Division. Kansas City would lose, 35–10, to the Green Bay Packers in Super Bowl I, but Davis was building a powerhouse.

"Al felt we were awfully close to being a great team but lacked a few things," said Scotty Stirling, who was general manager of the Raiders at the time. "So we went out and got them."

In 1966 the Raiders acquired cat-quick defensive tackle Tom Keating from the Buffalo Bills and tight end Hewritt Dixon, who was converted into a fullback, from the Denver Broncos.

Out of the draft, guard Jim Harvey and linebacker Bill Laskey became starters, and Pete Banaszak became a valuable reserve running back.

And 1967 was even better. Oakland made four big additions, bringing in three players who would eventually be enshrined in the Hall of Fame and another who would become the key to Oakland's vertical passing game.

Cornerback Willie Brown came from Denver, kicker-quarterback George Blanda from the Houston Oilers, and guard Gene Upshaw was the Raiders' number one draft choice from Texas A&I.

When Davis was signing those NFL quarterbacks, he had big, strong-armed Roman Gabriel of the Los Angeles Rams earmarked for Oakland. The merger forced all players signed by the rival league back to their original teams, but Davis eventually got a younger quarterback with a stronger arm than Gabriel's.

Tom Keating gets into the gap and pressures quarterback Pete Beathard of Houston.

Daryle Lamonica had been backing up Jack Kemp in Buffalo and was the Bills' quarterback of the future until being traded to Oakland with wide receiver Glenn Bass for quarterback Tom Flores and wide receiver Art Powell.

"I played with Daryle in Buffalo and I knew what he could do, so when they made the trade, I knew that it was going to help our team," Keating said. "He could really throw the ball.

"That being said, I don't know if anybody realized he would play as well as he did. I know I didn't."

Lamonica was born to throw the football. He could throw 50-yard spirals with the flick of his wrist. He could throw the deep out, the corner, and the post with more than enough mustard on the football.

In 1969 Lamonica threw an 80-yard touchdown pass to Warren Wells in the closing minutes to beat the San Diego Chargers. Wells was nearing the San Diego 10 yard line when he caught the ball.

During an era when the best high school quarterbacks in the nation wanted to play for Notre Dame, Lamonica had been the starting quarterback for the Fighting Irish.

"The thing I remember about Daryle, he would be windmilling his arm in the locker room and in the tunnel coming down to the field," Upshaw recalled. "He couldn't wait to start throwing the ball.

"He had a great arm and threw such beautiful passes. When he started throwing the ball deep in practice, everybody would stop and watch. They started calling him 'The Mad Bomber.'

"He could really throw the bomb, and he had a great year in '67."

Lamonica completed a modest 51.8 percent of his passes in 1967, but the Raiders were not looking for completions;

they wanted yards. Lamonica gave Oakland 3,228 of them and thirty touchdown passes in fourteen games.

He was the AFL's most valuable player.

"Al Davis believed in the vertical passing game," Lamonica said. "That's what we did, throw the ball down the field. We would rather hit a 15-yard pass, even if it took three tries, than three 5-yarders.

"We tried to dictate to the defense with our formations or motion. We saw mostly man-to-man defense in those days, and we felt any one of our receivers could get open one on one.

"We used all of our receivers and we used the whole field."

Dixon, who played fullback for the first time when he came to Oakland, joined Clem Daniels to form an explosive backfield and led the Raiders with fifty-nine receptions for 563 yards.

Wide receiver Fred Biletnikoff would become a possession receiver later in his career, but in 1967 he was a deep threat, catching forty passes for 876 yards—a 21.9 average—and five touchdowns.

Bill Miller, the other wide receiver, caught thirty-eight passes for 537 yards and six touchdowns. Tight end Billy Cannon was another deep threat with thirty-two catches for 629 yards and ten touchdowns.

Wells was just starting to blossom into the brilliant receiver he would become, catching thirteen passes for 302 yards and a 23.2 average, and he took six of them for touchdowns.

Upshaw solidified a line that included center Jim Otto and guard Wayne Hawkins, the last two survivors from the Raiders' first season in 1960. Otto, the only All-AFL center in the league's ten years of existence, was perhaps the best center of all time.

"In 1967 Otto might have had the best year any center ever had," Stirling said. "He just understood what defenses were doing. He was really good at picking up the blitz. Part of it was instinct; he seemed to know where they were coming from.

"Upshaw was just an incredible athlete playing on the offensive line. He was big, strong, fast, and he was obviously very bright. And he was very durable. I don't ever remember him being hurt.

Gene Upshaw holds a sign of the times at Super Bowl XI.

Gene Upshaw

When the Oakland Raiders made their first pick in the 1967 draft, the first draft to combine American Football League and National Football League selections, it was met with a unified response: "Who is Eugene Upshaw?"

Upshaw was a 6'5", 260-pound small college All-American from Texas A&I who would lay the foundation of what NFL Films would later call the greatest line in NFL history.

Not only would Upshaw fill a gaping hole in the Raiders' offensive line, he would give Oakland an answer to defensive tackle Buck Buchanan of the archrival Kansas City Chiefs and go on to become perhaps the best pulling guard ever.

"They gave Lamonica time to throw and he had that magnificent arm."

Lamonica knew it would take more than offense, however.

"We had a great offense and we could score a lot of points, but you win championships with defense," Lamonica said. "We played great defense that year."

Not only that, his leadership skills would soon become evident. Upshaw became offensive captain and player representative of the Raiders, and later president of the NFL Players Association. After retiring in 1981, he would become executive director of the NFLPA.

Among the enduring snapshots of Upshaw are of him raising the game balls in victory after Super Bowls XI and XV.

If center Jim Otto was the heart of the Raiders, Upshaw was the pride.

Before a playoff game against the Kansas City Chiefs in 1968, Upshaw went to the center of the field for the coin toss. The Chiefs won the toss and rather than take the ball, Coach Hank Stram had decided to defend the South goal to take advantage of a strong wind and rely on his powerful defense.

In those days the team winning the toss could not defer its decision until the second half, so in essence the Chiefs were challenging the Raiders' offense, which would get the ball at the start of each half.

Upshaw couldn't believe his ears.

"You what?" he asked middle linebacker Willie Lanier, the Kansas City captain, just to make sure he had heard the Chiefs' decision correctly.

When the realization sunk in, Upshaw was fuming.

"You'll regret this," he told Lanier, and he yelled the same thing toward Stram on the Kansas City sideline.

When Upshaw returned to the Oakland sideline, he told his teammates, "Buckle up your chinstraps. We've just been insulted."

Thus inspired, the Raiders scored three touchdowns in the first quarter and routed the Chiefs behind Daryle Lamonica's five touchdown passes, 41–6.

The Raiders opened their 13–1 season with a 51–0 victory over the Denver Broncos and then routed the Boston Patriots, 35–7, before facing perhaps their three most difficult regular-season games.

The defense would win two of them.

The defending champion Chiefs came to Oakland and left with a 23–21 setback, as the balance of power in the AFL's Western Division began to shift.

The Raiders went to New York for a Saturday night game and suffered their only defeat of the regular season, 27–14, to the Jets before bouncing back with a 24–20 victory at Buffalo over the three-time defending Eastern Division champion Bills.

Lamonica's return to Buffalo was the pregame storyline.

"I talked with [owners] Ralph Wilson Sr. and Jr. the day before I was traded to Oakland, and they both told me I had a chance to beat out Kemp that year," Lamonica said. "There was no talk of a trade. I was out hunting the next day, and when I came back, I learned I had been traded.

"I drove to Oakland the following day, and I circled the game at Buffalo on my calendar. I started to prepare for it that day. I remember [cornerback] Butch Byrd said I wouldn't throw a touchdown on his side of the field, and I threw two in the first half."

But the game was a defensive struggle, and Lamonica had to be happy he wasn't playing quarterback for the Bills.

The Raiders, who would set a pro football record with sixty-seven sacks that season, were all over Kemp, sacking the future congressman eleven times.

"That set the tempo for the whole year," Tom Keating said. "It was just a footrace to see who would get back there first. A few weeks later, we had twelve sacks against Denver and knocked [quarterback] Steve Tensi out of the game.

"It was just so much fun. We got some momentum and just kept on going. We had sixty-seven sacks that year for 666 yards, almost exactly 10 yards a crack. And with the offense scoring a lot of points, we just started to roll."

Sportswriter Larry Felser of the *Buffalo Evening News* watched the onslaught from the press box that day in War Memorial Stadium and wrote, "The Raiders play defense like eleven angry men."

The name stuck, and Bob Valli, the Raiders' beat writer for the *Oakland Tribune*, used the phrase "Eleven Angry Men of Defense" in almost every story he wrote for the rest of the season.

It all started with the front four of tackles Keating and Dan Birdwell and ends Big Ben Davidson and Ike Lassiter.

Much of the damage came from Oakland's "Over-30 Lou" defensive scheme, which had been a disaster during the preseason when the Raiders were routed by the Chiefs, 55–0, at Portland, Oregon, and beaten, 21–16, by the woeful Broncos at North Platte, Nebraska.

In the "Over-30 Lou," the Raiders would move one of their tackles out to end and put the other on the nose of the center.

"I hated playing outside and I don't think I was very good there, either," said Keating, a 6'2", 250-pounder, who was probably the quickest defensive tackle in football. "I didn't complain, but after the preseason, I was glad when they told me Danny was going to play outside from then on.

"The advantage, in those days, was that the center had a lot of other assignments and calls to make and was not used to having a man right over him. Centers were often the slowest of the linemen, and I could get a quick step on them.

"Back then, the officials didn't call you for getting in the neutral zone, so I would get really close to the center. The only drawback was a smart quarterback could get you to jump off-side. I remember Babe Parilli of Boston got me five times in the first half of one game.

"The guards would try to help block me, but they didn't know which way I was going, and sometimes all three guys would try to block me, leaving an opening for somebody else. I liked it if a guard would back up and wait for me because that would create a seam. Once I got in the gap between the guard and center, I was only two steps away from the quarterback.

"Danny and our ends were so good at getting pressure from the outside, the quarterback would step up in the pocket and we would just collapse it on him."

Lassiter was a 6'5", 270-pounder the Raiders signed as a free agent out of little St. Augustine College in 1965.

His favorite quarterback was Joe Namath of the Jets.

"Joe was real nice to you," said Lassiter, who once broke Namath's jaw with a vicious hit. "He would compliment you after a good hit. He used to grunt when you would hit him. I loved to hear that sound."

Davidson, 6'8" and 275 pounds, who came to the Raiders after stints with Green Bay and Washington in the NFL, was the best known of the group because of his movie career. He played in *M*A*S*H* and several other films and had a cameo as a bouncer in the porn classic, *Behind the Green Door*.

"I hung around after I shot my part [in *Green Door*] to see if they might ask me to stick around for some of the other filming, but no such luck," Davidson said with a twitch of his trademark handlebar mustache.

Big Ben had a mean streak on the field but was a pussycat off it. He once played Santa Claus for the children in an Oakland church group after their mothers sewed together a costume suited for a giant.

"We had the reputation that we were a bunch of thugs and ex-convicts," Davidson said. "Who knows what people thought of us?"

Davidson made a number of infamous hits on quarterbacks such as Len Dawson of the Kansas City Chiefs and Namath.

Once he knocked Namath into the goal post, which in those days was on the goal line.

"Namath was so still, I thought he might be dead," Keating said. "Ben would hit the quarterback as he was getting into the car with his girlfriend after the game. And to Ben, that wasn't a late hit."

Birdwell, 6'4" and 260 pounds, was one of the few holdovers from the dreary early days of the Raiders, having been a sixth-round draft choice out of Houston in 1962.

An excellent run stopper as well as a fine pass rusher, Birdwell also was the unchallenged standout on a team of characters.

"Danny was so hairy, it looked like he was wearing a sweater," Keating said. "After a game, he would lather up his face from the top of his chest, and he would shave it all off in about five quick strokes.

"Then he would slap on some aftershave lotion and walk out with blood all over his face. He would do this after every game."

Davidson told Keating before training camp in 1967 that the two of them couldn't room together anymore.

"Nothing personal, but it's Birdie," Davidson said. "Nobody will room with him because he smells so bad."

It wasn't poor hygiene, it was that Birdwell was partial to a pain-relieving and healing medication called DMSO. Wives and girlfriends wouldn't come close to a player who was using

DMSO to get over an injury. Birdwell used DMSO regularly for the normal football aches and pains.

"DMSO makes you smell like horses," Lassiter said. "You didn't even want to stand next to him in the huddle."

In fact Birdwell had good hygiene habits, as he proved to one rookie roommate during training camp. The rookie noticed that Birdwell did not have a toothbrush in the bathroom, and after several days curiosity got the best of him.

"Don't you brush your teeth?" the rookie asked.

Retorted Birdwell: "Of course, I brush three times a day."

"Then where's your toothbrush?" the rookie wanted to know.

Said Birdwell: "I've been using yours."

Birdwell was so versatile and athletic that the Raiders also were able to use him in pass coverage, which was another Oakland strength.

Willie Brown was on his way to the Hall of Fame, but until Kent McCloughan suffered a knee injury the following year, the Raiders were not sure which one was the better cornerback.

"They were both so good in the bump-and-run," Stirling said. "Willie was bigger and stronger, but McCloughan was almost a world-class sprinter at 60 yards and he was faster.

"Willie could pin guys to the sideline, and McCloughan could run with receivers all the way down the field. He had more trouble with a guy with moves. They covered so well, it gave our front four time to get to the quarterback."

The rest of the defenders were not as athletic, but linebackers Dan Conners and Gus Otto and safeties Warren Powers, Dave Grayson, and Howie Williams were all smart and tough. The Raiders added strong, athletic rookie linebacker Bill Laskey from Michigan to that group.

Oakland had built a team that was geared to challenge the Kansas City Chiefs. For example, Upshaw was drafted to block defensive tackle Buck Buchanan, and Brown was brought in to cover wide receiver Otis Taylor.

"The team was constructed to beat Kansas City," Stirling said. "We knew that if we were going anywhere, we had to beat the Chiefs. They were the best team in our division and our league.

"If you look at the record for the next few years, the Raiders dominated the Chiefs."

From 1967–70, the Raiders had an 8–2 record against the Chiefs, including two playoff games. It all started in the third game of 1967, when the defending champions came to Oakland.

As usual, when the Raiders and Chiefs played, it was a bruising game.

"We could play the first half without the ball and nobody would notice," Upshaw once said of the rivalry.

The Raiders held a 16–14 lead early in the fourth quarter and were driving for the clinching touchdown when Lamonica reached into the Oakland playbook for the back-breaking play.

It was a tight-end screen pass, which the Raiders had been saving for just such a situation.

"Billy Cannon had the speed to take a screen pass 80 yards for a touchdown, but that was tough to do against the Chiefs, so I didn't want to waste it," Lamonica said. "I didn't want to just get 20 or 30 yards in the middle of the field, I wanted to get a touchdown when we used it.

"The Chiefs knew we liked to throw for the end zone when we got inside the 40, so they would be playing back a little. It was the perfect time for it. I always liked to call the screen pass when we got closer to the goal line."

The Chiefs fell for it, except for linebacker Bobby Bell, who made a desperate dive for Cannon at the line of scrimmage but was unable to knock him off his feet.

Cannon ran 29 yards for a touchdown, and the Raiders held off a Kansas City rally for a 23–21 victory.

"We had beaten the Chiefs the year before in Kansas City, so we felt we could beat them again," said running back Clem Daniels. "We had added some guys, so we felt we were better than they were.

"Not only did we add good players, guys like George Blanda brought a winning mentality. Once we beat Kansas City, we knew we could beat everybody else in the league, because they were supposed to be the best."

Unfortunately, Daniels wouldn't be around until the end.

Daniels, the Raiders' most versatile threat as a tough runner and swift receiver out of the backfield, led Oakland that season with 575 yards rushing and caught sixteen passes for 222 yards and two touchdowns.

But he suffered a broken leg in the ninth game of the season, a 31–17 victory over the Miami Dolphins, and was lost for the year.

"I was pass blocking and our right tackle, Bob Svihus, was pushed back into me by defensive end Mel Branch," Daniels recalled. "I saw it coming but was just not able to get out of the way.

"We were having a great year and I knew we were going to the Super Bowl. Timing just was not on my side."

Rookie Pete Banaszak was inserted into the lineup, and although not nearly as fast as Daniels, he proved to be an able replacement. He rushed for 376 yards and caught sixteen passes for 192 yards.

The Raiders didn't miss a beat, routing the Chiefs, 44–22, the following week in Kansas City on Thanksgiving. Willie Brown and Warren Powers returned interceptions for touchdowns, allowing Oakland to finish the regular season with ten consecutive victories to claim its first division title.

The Houston Oilers, AFL Eastern Division champions, put up a good fight before losing to the Raiders, 19–0, during the regular season, but the AFL Championship Game was no contest.

Two play calls by Lamonica in the first half blew open a close game and led to a 40–7 Oakland victory.

The Raiders held a 3–0 lead early in the second quarter when Lamonica called an audible, changing the play at the line of scrimmage. Instead of throwing a pass, he handed off to Dixon, who got a block from Upshaw and ran 69 yards for a touchdown.

"I was playing games with their middle linebacker [Garland Boyette]," Lamonica said. "He was coming on a blitz and stepped up into the two-hole. We ran a quick trap through the three-hole and Hewritt popped through clean. He was 15 yards downfield before anybody realized it, and he ran all the way down the hash marks."

Dixon finished the day with 144 yards and Banaszak added 116 as the Raiders went against their tendencies rushing for 263 yards with a chilly wind blowing and temperatures in the 40s.

Lamonica completed only ten of twenty-four passes for 111 yards and two touchdowns, one a 17-yarder to tight end Dave Kocourek on a fake field goal with eighteen seconds left in the first half for a 17–0 lead.

"They were all yelling, 'Look out for the fake,' as we were lining up, so I stayed down just a little longer than usual,"

Lamonica said. "Their left end came hard trying for the block and I got around him easily.

"Kocourek was all alone and that broke it open. We coasted after that."

The Raiders headed for the Super Bowl at Miami, training outside of town at St. Andrews Episcopal School for Boys in Boca Raton, where Blanda's extra points sailed into a marsh populated by alligators.

The media attention for the Super Bowl was only a fraction of what it would become. There were no mass interviews in hotel conference rooms and few press conferences. Some writers showed up at the Raiders' hotel and saw a few players on a balcony. The writers yelled the names of players they wanted to come down for interviews.

Scotty Stirling was busy taking ring sizes of the Raiders for what would turn out to be an AFL Championship ring. Dan Birdwell took a look at the bare metal of the sizing rings Stirling had and thought that was what the finished rings were going to look like.

"That's pretty chintzy looking for a Super Bowl ring," he said.

As it turned out, the Raiders would not get a Super Bowl ring in 1967, losing to Green Bay, 33–14, in legendary Vince Lombardi's last game as coach of the Packers.

But Lombardi, who said there were several teams in the NFL better than the Raiders, and reporters covering the game might have lost in the final score what actually happened on the field.

One writer said it might take ten years for an AFL team to beat one from the NFL.

"It wasn't like they pushed us all over the field," Keating said. "They didn't beat us physically. We made some mistakes

Hewritt Dixon (35) finds running room against Green Bay in Super Bowl II at Miami.

and they played solid. I guess you might expect that to happen since they were the champions and we were the upstarts.

"But the game was a lot closer than the score."

Keating had two and a half of Oakland's four sacks and was the best defensive lineman on the field that day. Dixon rushed for 54 yards and would have had more, but the Raiders were forced to abandon their running game in the second half.

The turning point came just before halftime. The Packers held a 13–7 lead and Blanda had just missed a 47-yard field goal attempt, but Oakland forced Green Bay to punt from its 15 yard line.

Rodger Bird, a sure-handed returner all season, fumbled the punt near midfield, and the Packers recovered on the Oakland 45. Instead of the Raiders having a chance to inch closer with a field goal or take the lead with a touchdown, Don

Chandler kicked a 43-yard field goal and the Packers led at halftime, 16–7.

The Packers scored ten unanswered points in the third quarter, and Lamonica, who threw two touchdown passes to Miller, was forced to take some chances trying to catch up. Herb Adderley intercepted one of his passes and returned it 60 yards for a touchdown.

"The Packers weren't any better than I expected them to be, but I expected them to be great, the best in pro football," Lamonica said.

Daryle Lamonica threw two touchdown passes against the Packers in Super Bowl II.

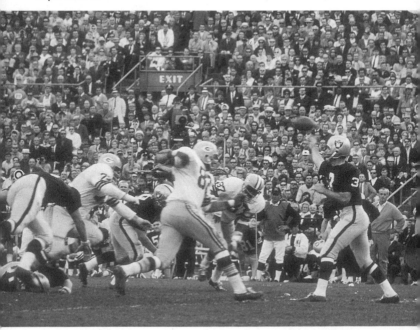

The Raiders probably lost their best chance to exploit the Packer defense when Daniels went down in the ninth week of the season. His speed coming out of the backfield might have caused problems for Green Bay's big linebackers.

"Rooster [Banaszak] was a tough, hard-running back, but it took him a day and a half to run out of sight," Upshaw said in 2002. "Clem could do some things that they might not have had an answer for.

"Clem had great hands and real speed coming out of the backfield. If Bobby Bell couldn't stay with him, I don't think the Packers' linebackers could have either, no matter how great they were."

Said Daniels: "For thirty years I've said they couldn't have handled us had I been able to play. We had so many weapons, but without me they were able to take away Billy Cannon, the only other deep speed we had.

"I've always felt we could have had a chance to win."

Banaszak was limited to 16 yards rushing, exactly 100 fewer than he had against Houston, although he did catch four passes for 69 yards—but he fumbled twice.

"I don't know what happened," said a tearful Banaszak, who grew up watching the Packers in Crivitz, Wisconsin. "I'm not a fumbler. Those guys were my heroes. It was like playing against your father."

Banaszak was one of the few Raiders who would get a chance for redemption in the Super Bowl, though it would take nine years. He scored two touchdowns as the Raiders beat Minnesota in Super Bowl XI.

The NFL would learn how good the upstart AFL was in Super Bowl III, but unfortunately for the Raiders, it was the New York Jets who showed them.

Heidi and the Jets

Despite a famous interlude with a little girl named Heidi, what was supposed to be a fairytale season for the Oakland Raiders in 1968 turned into a nightmare.

NFL Films, with the help of ESPN Classic sports channel, has helped make the "Heidi Game," played in Oakland on November 17, 1968, one of the most famous games in National Football League history, but fans of the old American Football League know the real classic was played by the Raiders and Jets six weeks later in the AFL Championship Game.

Oakland, coming off a loss to the Green Bay Packers in Super Bowl II and the AFL favorite to return, scored two touchdowns in the final minutes of the first game after NBC cut away to show the scheduled movie, the children's classic *Heidi*, at 7:00 P.M. in the eastern time zone.

The Raiders won that game, 43–32, but the Jets won the game that counted the most, 27–23, on a Raider gaffe in the closing minutes. They went on to a date with destiny and the Baltimore Colts in Super Bowl III. Broadway Joe Namath guaranteed the Jets would win the Super Bowl and delivered a monumental 16–7 victory over the Colts at the Orange Bowl stadium in Miami, the first time a team from the upstart AFL defeated a team from the established NFL.

"That was great for the history of the game, but a part of me has always felt that should have been [the Raiders] who were the first AFL team to do it," said John Madden, who was an assistant with the Raiders in 1968, before taking over as head coach when John Rauch went to the Buffalo Bills as coach and general manager in 1969.

"On the other hand, since it wasn't us, I'm glad it was Joe Namath and the Jets. We were rooting for them because of the whole AFL-NFL thing. That game changed pro football. But I will always believe we would have beaten the Colts, too."

There are many people who followed the AFL who also believe it, especially after watching heavily favored Baltimore sleepwalk through the first half of the Super Bowl.

With the Jets holding a 7–0 lead over the bumbling Colts at intermission, sportswriter Larry Felser of the *Buffalo Evening News* said in the press box loud enough for all the writers covering NFL teams to hear: "It's a good thing the Oakland Raiders aren't here or you wouldn't be able to find the Colts."

But the Raiders were watching the Super Bowl on television with the rest of the world because a throw that quarterback Daryle Lamonica meant to be a pass to rookie running back Charlie Smith wound up as a lateral.

Namath, tired of all the talk during Super Bowl week that the Jets had no chance against the Colts, told writers: "We're going to win. I guarantee it."

After the game, he told them why.

"The big one was winning the AFL Championship Game," he said. "Once we beat the Raiders, we knew we could beat the Colts."

The Raiders had a 21–13–2 edge in the all-time series with the Jets, including playoffs, through 2002, but it still sticks in the craw of Oakland fans that the Jets won the biggest game of all on December 29, 1968.

A brutally cold and windy day didn't prevent Lamonica and Namath from filling the raw winter air with footballs. Lamonica completed twenty of forty-seven passes for 401 yards and a touchdown. Namath completed nineteen of forty-nine for 266 yards and three scores.

Namath picked on rookie cornerback George Atkinson, who was trying to cover Don Maynard—a future Pro Football Hall of Fame wide receiver—who caught six passes for 118 yards and two touchdowns.

The Raiders held a 23–20 lead when Namath hit Maynard in the back of the end zone for a 6-yard touchdown with 7:47 remaining to give New York a 27–23 advantage.

"We know Atkinson is going to be a good player," Namath said after the game. "But we have a veteran going against a rookie and we felt we could take advantage of his inexperience."

The Raiders weren't quite finished.

Lamonica completed passes of 24 yards to Fred Biletnikoff and 37 yards to Warren Wells, and the Jets were penalized for a personal foul to put the ball on the New York 12 yard line with a little more than two minutes remaining.

Ben Davidson sacks quarterback Joe Namath of the New York Jets.

Fred Biletnikoff

When Fred Biletnikoff lost his pre-game meal in the locker room, the Oakland Raiders knew he was ready to play.

Biletnikoff got sick before virtually every game he ever played.

"When we heard Freddie getting sick, we knew he was OK," Gene Upshaw said. "If he didn't, then we might get worried."

Biletnikoff, most valuable player of Super Bowl XI and a member of the Pro Football Hall of Fame, also had a way of making defensive backs look sick.

Fred Biletnikoff set up three touchdowns in Super Bowl XI.

From 1965–78 Biletnikoff caught 589 passes, and his smooth moves and unerring hands made him perhaps the best possession receiver in pro football history, even though he was afraid he might be cut as a rookie.

"When I got to Oakland, I had to beat somebody really good to get open each time," Biletnikoff recalled. "I tended to get so hung up trying to beat my man, I had trouble catching the football."

Which is sort of like Rembrandt having trouble painting.

Biletnikoff dropped five passes in his first exhibition game for the Raiders before holding on to a throw from quarterback Lee Grosscup that went 80 yards for a touchdown.

A perfectionist, the sure-handed Biletnikoff once dropped a pass during training camp and was so angry he knocked down 50 yards of a portable fence that separated two practice fields.

Not that he needed any help holding onto the ball, but Biletnikoff took no chances, applying now-outlawed stickum not only on his hands and arms but much of his body.

"When he caught a ball, you couldn't use it any more," Kenny Stabler said. "[Center] Jim Otto would go to the line to snap the ball for the next play, but he wouldn't touch the ball until they gave him a new one.

"Freddy would tape his forearms and spray all this sticky stuff on them. Then he would apply stickum on his socks, his jersey, everywhere. And he would put more on as the game went along."

Despite that, defensive backs just couldn't stick with him.

In the huddle Lamonica called a play the Raiders had worked on all week and saved for just such a situation.

"We saw a weakness in their defense that we thought we could take advantage of," Lamonica recalled. "We put in a quick screen to Charlie Smith, like a flare pass. We practiced it all week and thought it would be a big play for us."

The timing was off from the start, however, and Lamonica floated the ball over Smith's head into the right flat—a throw that was ruled to be a lateral. Linebacker Ralph Baker scooped up the ball, and in a New York minute the Jets were on their way to Miami.

"Charlie got turned around a little and I had to get rid of the ball," Lamonica says. "I called the play and I threw the ball, so I take responsibility. But the play was there. If we had executed, I think we would have scored a touchdown. I'd call the same play again.

"If I could have one throw back in my career, that would be it."

Smith was a 6'1", 210-pound running back chosen in the fourth round out of Utah State in the brilliant Raider draft of 1968 that included quarterback Kenny Stabler, tackle Art Shell, defensive back George Atkinson, fullback Marv Hubbard, and linebacker Chip Oliver.

The Raiders needed a replacement for Clem Daniels, their great running back who doubled as a deep receiver, because a knee injury in 1967 virtually ended his career.

Smith fit the mold perfectly.

"It was great coming to the Raiders and not just because I was from Oakland," said Smith, a graduate of Castlemont High who was so fast he once beat Jimmy Hines of McClymonds High, a future Olympic gold-medal winner, in the 100-yard dash.

"I could run and I could always catch. The Raiders took advantage of all my skills. They used me coming out of the backfield to keep defensive backs honest. And I was a blocker. I sometimes wish we could have run the ball more, but it was a pleasure to play in that offense."

Smith became a starter that season, rushing for 504 yards and six touchdowns and catching twenty-two passes for 321 yards and two more touchdowns.

Like Lamonica, he vividly remembers the lateral against the Jets, and he believes there was a culprit.

"It was the wind," Smith said. "Parts of the field were frozen because it was so cold, and the wind was really blowing, gusting. There were a lot of incomplete passes that day because the ball just took off in the wind.

"When Daryle threw the ball, he was behind me and I was already thinking of what I was going to do once I caught it because I knew there would be a linebacker there to try to cover me. But by the time the ball got to me, I had to turn all the way around to try to catch it. At the last minute, it went behind me, and when the ball hit the ground, the wind carried it back down the field.

"I was off balance and had to gather myself, but by the time I did, they already had the ball. That was it."

But it was the Raiders who had left the Jets wondering what happened the first time the teams met that season.

Curiously, Lamonica and Smith also were the central figures for the Raiders in that game. It was a classic AFL shootout that included eight lead changes and ties, with Lamonica and Namath taking turns leading remarkable scoring drives that entertained a capacity crowd at the Oakland Coliseum and a national television audience.

Jim Turner, nicknamed the "Crockett Rocket" because he

hailed from the tiny port city of Crockett, not far from Oakland, kicked a 26-yard field goal — his fourth of the game — to give New York a 32–29 lead.

Turner, who played at Utah State, was out of football in 1964 when he had a tryout with the Jets after a game at Frank Youell Field in Oakland. The Jets signed him, and he joined the team for the flight back to New York.

Turner's six-year career with the Jets was very productive, particularly when he kicked three field goals to provide the winning margin against Baltimore in Super Bowl III. When NFL Commissioner Pete Rozelle walked into the New York dressing room after that game, Turner yelled: "Hey, Pete. Welcome to the AFL."

Turner kicked off after his fourth field goal of the game against the Raiders in 1968, and Smith returned the ball to the Oakland 23 yard line. NBC cut to a commercial and never came back to the game in the eastern time zone, switching to another classic, *Heidi*, instead.

What the fans in the East missed in the final minute were two touchdowns by the Raiders, but actually, the Raiders reached the end zone three times.

First, Lamonica hit Smith circling out of the backfield and splitting the middle of the Jets' defense. The speedy rookie took the ball for an apparent 67-yard touchdown that was nullified by a penalty.

"I will always remember Johnny Sample, who played cornerback for the Jets, coming up to me and saying, 'Nice try, Lamonica. Better luck next year,' " Lamonica said.

But the Raiders had more where that came from.

Lamonica hit Smith for 20 yards, and the Raiders picked up 15 more when safety Mike D'Amato brought him down with a face-mask tackle, putting the ball on the New York 43 yard line.

D'Amato was replacing starting safety Jim Hudson, who had been ejected early in the game. The Raiders went back to that matchup on the next play and Smith caught Lamonica's pass before outrunning D'Amato down the right sideline to the end zone.

"I would have outrun Hudson, too," Smith said. "The play that was called back was a circle pattern, but teams were getting wise to that. So on the touchdown, I ran to the hash mark on the right side and then broke to the sideline.

"That play was open all day, but Daryle told me to be patient, that we would get to it. Our wide receivers ran deep patterns to clear out the secondary and then I just cut underneath."

The Raiders had a 36–32 lead but added to it nine seconds later when Earl Christy fumbled the kickoff, and free-agent rookie running back Preston Ridlehuber made himself a place in Raider lore by recovering in the end zone.

Ridlehuber is the answer to the ultimate Raider trivia question: "Who scored the last touchdown in the Heidi Game?"

The Raiders had won, but most people on the East Coast didn't know it yet.

Coach Weeb Ewbank of the Jets had a telephone call waiting for him when he reached the locker room in the bowels of the Coliseum.

"Congratulations," his wife said cheerily.

Retorted Ewbank: "What do you mean? We lost."

Ewbank angrily slammed down the phone, but later he regained his sense of humor. When informed of NBC's gaffe, he quipped: "I also think the game should have ended right after Turner's field goal put us ahead.

"It was a hard-fought game but we all got out alive, so I guess you could call it a Mexican victory."

But not for NBC.

Dick Cline, the network's broadcast operations supervisor, tried to explain what happened.

"[Prior to the game] it was determined that *Heidi* would air at 7 o'clock," Cline said. "If football wasn't over, we would still go to *Heidi* at 7 o'clock. So I waited and I waited and I heard nothing. We came up to that magic hour and I thought, 'Well, I haven't been given any counterorder, so I've got to do what we agreed to do.' "

Unbeknownst to Cline, NBC officials watching what was turning into the game of the year on their televisions at home got together on a telephone hookup and made a decision with seven minutes left to air the remainder of the game to the East

Coast and delay the start of *Heidi*. But thousands of calls to NBC from concerned viewers inquiring about the game and *Heidi* jammed the switchboard, and in those days before cell phones, Cline never got the call.

"People began calling before 7 o'clock saying one of two things," said former NBC executive Chet Simmons. " 'What are you going to do about *Heidi*?' Or, 'Don't let the game go on.' What it did was, it literally blew out the switchboard."

The Heidi Game wound up having a major impact on the future of TV sports programming. The NFL inserted language into its television contracts guaranteeing that games of visiting clubs would be shown to their home markets in their entirety.

"Probably the most significant factor to come out of *Heidi* was, whatever you do, you better not leave an NFL football game," says Val Pinchbeck, the NFL's retired chief of broadcasting.

"Ten years earlier, if you did the same thing on a telecast, would you get the same type of an uproar? I don't know. But you sure did at that point in time. It sure let you know that you better not take my football away from me at 7 o'clock."

Finally, calls from irate football fans overloaded NBC's switchboard and it broke down completely.

About twenty minutes after the game, NBC ran a "crawl" at the bottom of the screen telling viewers who were watching *Heidi* that the Raiders had won the game, 43–32.

NBC president Julian Goodman released a statement ninety minutes after the game.

"It was a forgivable error committed by humans who were concerned about children expecting to see *Heidi* at 7:00 P.M.," read the statement. "I missed the end of the game as much as anyone else."

The Heidi Game was voted the most memorable regular-season game in NFL history and one of the ten most memorable of all time in a 1997 media poll taken in conjunction with the NFL's 10,000th regular-season game.

Because of the blown switchboard, many fans could not get through to NBC to complain. Instead, they began calling the New York City Police Department and the New York Telephone Company.

"It was on the front page of the *New York Times*," Simmons said. "And when you say something is on the front page of the *New York Times*, you've got to figure it's pretty important."

Those 1968 classics were just two of the many memorable games played between the Jets and the Raiders.

Lamonica got a small measure of revenge on December 6, 1970, at Shea Stadium, when he threw a 33-yard touchdown pass to Warren Wells with one second remaining to give the Raiders a 14–13 victory. Wells was blanketed by defensive backs Earlie Thomas and Steve Tannen, but the Oakland receiver reached between the defenders and tipped the ball to the back of the end zone, where only he could get it.

"That was one of the greatest plays and greatest catches I've ever seen," Lamonica said. "It was all or nothing. I just had to throw the ball into the end zone and hope."

Lamonica and Namath put on another show on December 11, 1972, before the *Monday Night Football* cameras at Oakland.

Namath completed twenty-five of forty-six passes for 403 yards and a touchdown, but the Raiders walked off with a 24–16 victory.

"What I remember about that game was Namath was sacked by Art Thoms and practically had to be carried off the

Daryle Lamonica passed for 401 yards against the Jets in the 1968 AFL Championship Game.

field," said Raiders' executive assistant Al LoCasale, who has been with the organization since 1969. "It looked like he was through for the night. But the next time the Jets got the ball, he came limping back out onto the field and 50,000 fans in Oakland gave him a standing ovation."

Despite that feel-good moment, there was plenty of bad blood in the rivalry.

The Raiders' Ike Lassiter once broke Namath's jaw with a hit, even though fellow defensive end Ben Davidson got the blame because of a famous picture taken in that game in which he knocked off Namath's helmet.

Namath refused to give either credit.

"I ate a tough piece of steak in the pregame meal," Joe Willie told reporters through a swollen cheek after the game.

Maynard caught seven passes for 131 yards in that Monday night game to become pro football's all-time leading receiver at the time. Then, in the fourth quarter, linebacker Phil Villapiano of the Raiders delivered a shot that broke Maynard's nose.

Several of the Jets called it a cheap shot, but Villapiano swears it was an accident.

"When I was a rookie, we were playing Kansas City in the [next-to-last] game of the season," said Villapiano, who grew up in New Jersey watching the Jets. "I didn't check Otis Taylor at the line on a big play near the end of the game, and he caught a pass to set up a field goal that beat us and knocked us out of the playoffs. I made up my mind that nobody would do that to me again.

"On the play against Maynard, I went out to check him and he tried to juke me. He had that single-bar face mask. I was wearing gloves with pads inside and hit him right in the face, but I was just trying to jam him.

"Weeb Ewbank came running out there screaming and yelling. George Atkinson told him to get off the field. That's just the way it was. It was the Jets and the Raiders."

Lamonica remembers it this way: "We were the power in the West and they were the power in the East, so it was sort of a natural rivalry. New York is the media capital, so when you are playing a New York team, a lot of people are paying attention.

"We had some great games. It was more than me against Namath when we played, but he was always the kind of guy you tried to measure up to. I definitely got up for those games to play against him and show what I had. Everybody remembers the Heidi Game, but it was just one of many."

Frank Ramos, the Jets' longtime director of public relations, probably put it the best: "When the Jets played the Raiders, it wasn't a rivalry. It was a war."

Replay It Again

The Oakland Raiders have a history with instant replay, and it's all bad.

The Raiders were involved in what many observers feel was the first game in which National Football League officials used instant replay to determine the outcome of a play, and ultimately, a game.

The Raiders were involved in the game that is considered the flashpoint for the NFL instituting its first instant replay policy.

The Raiders were involved in probably the most controversial game in NFL history in which instant replay overturned a call on the field.

The Raiders lost all three decisions and all three games in the NFL playoffs.

Those incidents have come to be known as the Immaculate Reception, Rob Lytle's Fumble That Wasn't, and the Tuck Play.

The Pittsburgh Steelers used Franco Harris's "Immaculate Reception" to defeat the Raiders, 13–7, at Three Rivers Stadium on December 23, 1972, on what NFL Films has declared the most famous play in NFL history. It is believed that replay was used to try to determine exactly what happened on the play.

The Denver Broncos took advantage of a fumble by Lytle that was not called by officials and scored a touchdown on the next play to beat the Raiders, 20–17, in the 1977 American Football Conference Championship Game at Mile High

Charles Woodson (24) separated the ball from Tom Brady in the 2001 playoffs, but it was ruled an incomplete pass. (Brian Snyder/Reuters)

Stadium. The NFL instituted its first instant replay the following season.

The New England Patriots went on to win the Super Bowl after instant replay was used to overturn an apparent fumble by quarterback Tom Brady, who rallied the Patriots to a 16–13 overtime victory over the Raiders in the 2001 playoffs.

Replay and some still pictures suggest Brady had both hands on the ball, which he lost when he was hit by Charles Woodson, but officials invoked the "tuck rule" to call it an incomplete pass and not a fumble.

Lytle has admitted that he fumbled, and Brady said as much with his actions and words at the time.

But Frenchy Fuqua of the Steelers has never told exactly what happened on the Immaculate Reception. Fuqua seemed ready to tell in the locker room after the game but was hushed by Steeler officials.

Owner Art Rooney later told Fuqua, "Let's keep it 'Immaculate,' " and so he has.

Terry Bradshaw's pass on the play that was intended for Fuqua was broken up on a vicious hit by safety Jack Tatum of the Raiders. Under the rules of the day in the NFL, a pass could not be ruled complete if touched consecutively by two offensive players.

Tatum said he never touched the ball before it ended up in Harris's hands for a miraculous touchdown. Fuqua has threatened to tell several times but has kept his secret.

"I've seen Fuqua several times at golf tournaments or banquets, and we're always dogging him about it," said Phil Villapiano, a linebacker for the Raiders who was on the field for the play. "He just laughs and says, 'I'll never tell.' "

The NFL Films tape of what it has called "The Greatest Play in NFL History," which was replayed thousands of times even before the ESPN Classic and the NFL channels existed, is inconclusive.

Three Rivers Stadium, where the drama played out, was imploded in February 2001, and the Raiders and their fans were not unhappy to see it go.

Quarterback Kenny Stabler ran 30 yards for a touchdown to give Oakland a 7–6 lead with 1:13 remaining in a bitter defensive struggle. The Steelers, who would capture four Super Bowls later in the decade but had not yet won a playoff game in their forty-year history, were facing fourth down and 10 on the Pittsburgh 40 yard line.

Bradshaw dropped back to pass, but was almost immediately under pressure from the Raiders' front four. Defensive ends Tony Cline and Horace Jones actually got hands on him. But Bradshaw escaped and rifled a pass 25 yards down the middle toward Fuqua.

The ball and Tatum, the most feared hitter in the NFL, reached Fuqua in the same instant and there was a violent collision. It was Tatum's third spectacular pass breakup on that series of downs and as the ball caromed away, he and the Raiders began to celebrate—prematurely as it turned out.

"The last thing we said in the huddle is, 'Look, we got this game won,' " said George Atkinson, Tatum's partner at safety. " 'All we got to do is knock the ball down.' And guess what happens . . . Tate went for the big knockout."

The ball ricocheted toward Harris, the Steelers' rookie fullback, who was trailing the play. Harris caught the ball off his shoe tops at the Oakland 42 and raced down the sideline past Raider cornerback Jimmy Warren for a touchdown with five seconds left and into football lore.

"Going into the huddle, I was thinking how great a year it had been, and if this was going to be the last play, I was going to play it all the way out," Harris said. "Unfortunately, the play that was called didn't really involve me at all. I was supposed to stay in and block a linebacker if they blitzed, but they didn't.

"I knew Brad was in serious trouble, so I went downfield in case he needed me as an outlet receiver. I was always taught to go to the ball, so when he threw it, that's what I did. The next thing I knew, the ball was coming right to me.

"The rest has always been a blur. It happened so fast. It was all reaction. My only thought was to get to the end zone. It's amazing to me that this play has stood the test of time."

Villapiano was covering Harris but reacted to the pass and was not in position to make a play on the deflection. He thought he might tackle Harris, but Villapiano claims he was clipped by tight end John McMakin.

The tape indicates he might be right.

"I was right with Franco, but after Bradshaw threw the ball I went over to help out," Villapiano said. "The ball went over my head to Franco. Had I stayed where I was, it would have been right to me.

"I saw exactly what happened and made a move to cut Franco off. But McMakin dove on the back of my legs. It was blatant clipping. He always was a smart player and it was a great play, but he never gets any credit."

When Harris reached the end zone, confusion reigned.

Referee Fred Swearingen consulted with his officiating crew, then he went into the baseball dugout and got on the telephone with Art McNally, the NFL's supervisor of officials.

In the press box an announcement was made that officials were viewing videotape even though the league had no instant replay procedure at the time. NFL officials later denied it, but many people believe that was the first time replay was used to

Jack Tatum (31) broke up the pass intended for Frenchy Fuqua, but Franco Harris (32) turned the play into the "Immaculate Reception."

determine the outcome of a play. There also was a television monitor in the dugout near Swearingen.

Several minutes later, Swearingen reemerged and signaled for the first time that it was a touchdown.

"What bothered me about it then still bothers me now," said John Madden, coach of the Raiders. "If it was a touchdown, why didn't they call it a touchdown right away? If [Swearingen] didn't know it was a touchdown when it happened, how did he know it was a touchdown after he went over and talked on the phone?

"It doesn't go away, so there's never been any closure. I've never gotten over it and I never will. I have seen guys joke about it, but I never have. Just like that, our whole season, everything we worked for, was over. It's just something you have to live with.

"Unlike those other plays, we never had a chance after that to win the game."

There is only one replay that appears to show conclusively what happened, but it has rarely been seen. Tape taken by the end zone camera behind Bradshaw, when it is stopped at the moment of impact, shows the ball seemingly flatten out on Fuqua's left forearm.

Perhaps the only time that replay was shown on television was when NBC, which televised the game, ran the credits over it after the game.

Al LoCasale, a Raider executive since 1969, gets credit for supplying the punch line to a story about Swearingen's conversation on the phone.

LoCasale, who saw the play from the Oakland sideline, first told the story at an off-season banquet soon after the game, and like the Immaculate Reception, the joke has developed a life of its own.

"I said [Swearingen] asked how many cops there were to escort the officials out of the stadium if they didn't call it a touchdown," LoCasale said. "When he was told there were only six, he raised his arms and said, 'That's right. It's six for Pittsburgh.'

"Fuqua started talking about it in the locker room and they told him to shut up. It's hard to believe it was thirty years ago. It still hurts. I had a great view of the play and I'm sure the ball never hit Tatum."

Tatum wasn't even covering Fuqua on the play, having been assigned to shadow McMakin, but he reacted instinctively when he saw Bradshaw throw the ball.

Although acknowledging that tape he has seen is inconclusive, Tatum believes there is no way the ball could have touched him.

"Frenchy was between me and the ball, so if the ball hit me, it would have had to come through him or over the top of him and that didn't happen," Tatum said. "It's thirty years later and it doesn't really matter any more, but I never thought the ball hit me.

"George [Atkinson] has a funny take in it. He says we put Franco in the Hall of Fame."

Rooney, original owner of the Steelers, didn't see the play because he figured the game was lost and was on his way to the locker room to congratulate his players on the team's best season to date.

When he got downstairs, he learned of the touchdown but had to wait out the review.

"We should have gotten that game, but to Mr. Rooney's credit he got it, even though he was in the elevator and didn't see it," said Raider owner Al Davis. "We feel we were taken. It was a mistake, but I guess it was an honest mistake.

"Fuqua knows he hit it."

But he's still not saying.

That has never been the case with Lytle.

The Broncos were leading, 7–3, in the third quarter and were threatening for more when Lytle took the ball from quarterback Craig Morton on the 2 yard line. He lost it in the next instant when he was hit by, guess who, Jack Tatum.

"Of course, I fumbled," Lytle said, and all the replays showed clearly that he did.

Defensive tackle Mike McCoy of the Raiders came out of the pile with the football and was 50 yards downfield running for a possible touchdown when officials called him back. Officials gave the ball back to Denver on the 1 yard line.

On the next play fullback Jon Keyworth ran 1 yard for a touchdown, and the Broncos went on to victory as wide receiver Haven Moses had perhaps his best game as a pro with five catches for 168 yards and two touchdowns.

Afterward, Denver captain Billy Thompson presented the game ball to Moses and asked his teammates, "Who led us to the Promised Land?"

They chanted, "Moses, Moses."

Had you asked the same question in the Raiders' locker room, they probably would have said it was Fred Marion, the head linesman, who insisted Lytle did not fumble and would not even discuss it with the other officials on the crew.

"When the Broncos lined up and I saw the formation they were in, I knew they were going to run that play," Tatum said. "I read my keys and saw Lytle move to the middle and I knew he was going to get the ball. I shot the gap and got a real good hit on him. I saw the ball pop straight up in the air. It wasn't like the ball slid down and was hidden between all the bodies in there.

"My momentum carried us out of the way, and I remember when I got up everybody was running the other way and I thought we might get a touchdown. Then [Marion] came running in from the far side of the field and said Lytle was down. The two officials on our side said they knew it was a fumble, but the thing that got me was that he wouldn't even ask them.

"Then, two days later, the league admitted it was a bad call. Anybody who saw it knew that when it happened."

John Madden

The Miami Dolphins were credited for changing the face of defense in the National Football League with their "53" defense, which helped them win consecutive Super Bowls in 1972 and 1973.

The Dolphins would bring Bob Mathison, number 53, off the bench to replace a defensive lineman. Mathison was talented enough to rush the quarterback and defend the run like a defensive lineman or drop into pass coverage like a linebacker.

Opponents did not know until the ball was snapped if the Dolphins were in a standard 4–3 defense or a 3–4 alignment.

But Coach John Madden of the Oakland Raiders had been doing that for several years in his "Orange" defense with defensive linemen Dan Birdwell, Otis Sistrunk, and Tony Cline, who were agile enough to play pass defense.

"Miami has done great things with that defense, no question about it," Madden said at the time. "But I prefer the way we do it because our guys have been starters and are already on the field. We have the element of surprise because we can do it without giving anything away.

"Hank Stram did it in Kansas City, too, with Jerry Mays. You need a guy who is half defensive lineman and half linebacker. I think it's a big advantage when he's already on the field. The quarterback doesn't know when he's coming or when he's dropping off."

When Cline and two other starting linemen were injured during the 1976 season, the Raiders were forced to go with a 3–4 defense. However, Madden found a way to shift to a 4–3 without tipping his hand and used it effectively in the American Football Conference Championship Game against the Pittsburgh Steelers.

Monte Johnson, the Raiders' 250-pound middle linebacker, a defensive lineman in college at Nebraska, would move onto the line after the Steelers were set. Oakland shut down Pittsburgh's running game in a 24–7 victory.

Madden was also on the cutting edge of another developing trend when in the 1970s NFL coaches began to bring in specialists on offense and defense, depending on down and distance situations.

He even coined a name for it, "Situation Substitution."

"I remember [sports editor] George Ross wrote a big Sunday piece about 'Situation Substitution' in the *Oakland Tribune*," Madden said in 2002. "I knew it was going to be a big thing, but I had no idea it would become as big as it is. Now, you see four or five new players coming in on every play.

Coach John Madden went joyriding after Super Bowl XI.

"We also were one of the first teams to put thirteen or fourteen guys in the huddle. When we'd break the huddle, the extra guys would run off the field, but it would be too late. The defense didn't have time to adjust with its own substitutions.

"Then they voted that you could only have eleven players in the huddle. The Minnesota Vikings were the only other team that was putting extra guys in the huddle, so I knew Bud Grant and I were the only ones who would vote for it.

"So I voted against it because I knew we were going to lose."

Madden would send in defensive backs Neal Colzie and Charles Phillips in Oakland's nickel and dime defenses or pass rushers like Pat Toomay in obvious passing situations.

On offense Madden liked to use Mike Siani and Morris Bradshaw as extra wide receivers or Warren Bankston and Ted Kwalick in double- and triple- tight-end formations.

He's a thinker, not just the wild and crazy guy you see on TV.

Marion's call probably prevented a matchup made in football heaven in Super Bowl XII, the Raider Nation versus America's Team.

Instead, the Dallas Cowboys blew out the Broncos, 27–10, in one of the worst Super Bowls ever played.

Madden again was the victimized Raider coach.

"No matter how many times I watch the films of the Immaculate Reception, I never know for sure what happened," Madden wrote in his book, *Hey Wait a Minute (I Wrote a Book)*. "But the play in Denver was different. Films of that play confirmed what I knew had happened, that Rob Lytle of the Broncos had fumbled on our 1 yard line.

"The Broncos never should have scored on the next play and we never should have lost that game, 20–17. I knew all that without seeing the films, but Ed Marion didn't. But what annoyed me was that they never huddled. On the Immaculate Reception, at least the officials huddled. In Denver, they never did. If they had, I think one of the officials would have acknowledged that he had seen the fumble."

In 1983, after Madden had become the best football analyst on television, he was attending a preseason seminar for CBS Sports. Art McNally of the NFL was explaining rules of the game by showing game footage.

After each play, McNally would ask members of the audience what call should have been made on the play. After one play, McNally asked if it looked like a fumble.

Madden said he almost involuntarily blurted out: "What about the Rob Lytle play in Denver, the 1977 AFC Championship Game? Was that a fumble?"

The room was dark and Madden wasn't sure McNally realized who had asked the question.

"Yes, the Lytle play, that was a fumble," McNally said.

Madden responded: "Damn it, where the hell were you when I needed you? That call put the Broncos in the Super Bowl and we went home. That call gave me an ulcer."

As a direct result of the fallout from Lytle's fumble not being called, the NFL introduced a study on the use of instant replay as an officiating aid during seven nationally televised preseason games the following year.

In 1986 NFL owners approved a limited use of instant replay, and they have been tweaking it over the years.

Which brings us to the 2001 playoffs, and the tuck rule.

The Raiders held a 13–10 lead over the Patriots, who had the ball at the Oakland 48 yard line, with under two minutes remaining. Brady faded to pass but was hit by a blitzing Woodson and lost the football, which was recovered by linebacker Greg Biekert of the Raiders.

Game, set, match.

Because the Patriots had no timeouts remaining, all Raider quarterback Rich Gannon would have to do was to kneel down three times and the game would be over, advancing Oakland to the AFC Championship Game against the Pittsburgh Steelers.

But up in the replay booth, someone who has remained anonymous felt the play deserved another look.

Looking at the replay, all the announcers covering the game seemed to agree that the correct call had been made on the field.

That included former quarterback Phil Simms, who said he was certain it was a fumble.

The Raiders and Patriots apparently thought so, too. The Oakland players were celebrating, while Brady had picked himself up off the snow-covered field and trudged to the sideline with his head down.

Not one of the Patriots appealed to the officials that the play should have been ruled an incomplete pass.

However, referee Walt Coleman, who had made the original call, saw something different on the tape. After several minutes, Coleman ruled the play actually was an incomplete pass.

The ruling was based on Rule 3, Section 21, Article 2, Note 2 of the NFL rule book: "Any intentional forward movement of [the passer's] arm starts a forward pass, even if the player loses possession of the ball as he is attempting to tuck it back toward his body."

Explained Coleman to a pool reporter: "When I got over to the replay monitor and looked, it was obvious that his arm was coming forward, he was trying to tuck the ball and they just knocked it out of his hand. His hand was coming forward, which makes it an incomplete pass."

Asked what it would have taken for it to be ruled a fumble, Coleman said, "He would have had to have brought it all the way in and got it all the way underneath his arm in order for it [to be a fumble]."

The Patriots made several key first downs and Adam Vinatieri kicked a 45-yard field goal at the end of regulation to tie the score and a 23-yarder in overtime to give New England an unlikely 16–13 victory.

New England went on to upset Pittsburgh, 24–17, in the AFC title game and surprised the St. Louis Rams, 20–17, in the Super Bowl, when Vinatieri kicked a field goal on the last play of the game.

Brady didn't seem to know what to say when questioned about the disputed play after the game.

"Uh . . . ," Brady stammered. "You know, he hit me. I wasn't sure. Yeah, I was throwing the ball. How do you like that? Damn right. Damn right."

The Raiders were simply stunned by the call.

Pictures ran on the front pages of newspapers across the country the next day showing Brady with the ball in both hands the instant before he was leveled by Woodson.

"I thought it was a fumble, but the officials thought otherwise," said Coach Jon Gruden of the Raiders, who as it turned out was coaching his last game for Oakland. "It was obvious. You can never count on anything in the NFL. I don't understand how that play is looked at. But I thought it was a fumble."

So did practically everyone you asked.

Pictures usually don't lie, and from the first day football was played, if a player had both hands on the ball when he lost it, that was a fumble.

"It's bullshit," Woodson said. "I thought it was a bullshit call. It never should have been overturned. Unbelievable that [Coleman] could sit there and look at it that many times and still get the wrong call."

Faced with the public relations nightmare of an undeserving team still having a chance to win the Super Bowl, the NFL immediately turned to damage control.

Mike Pereira, the NFL's director of officiating, took a football with him the next day to an NFC playoff game in St. Louis because he knew he would be asked about the rule and wanted to be able to demonstrate.

He insisted the correct call was made.

"If you want to disagree with the rule, that's another thing," Pereira said. "Fans or media people may not like the rule, but it is a rule."

The tuck rule relieved officials of the burden of deciding a quarterback's intent when he brings his arm forward, Pereira said.

"Brady, at that point, was not trying to pass the ball, but it comes to his [left] hand," Pereira said. "He never controlled it long enough to consider him a runner, nor does he try to bring it up again to pass."

Among other things, that explanation begs the question, if he did not try to pass then how is it ruled an incomplete pass?

The answer never came.

"I think we did enough to win this game," wide receiver Jerry Rice of the Raiders told reporters. "It just didn't work out that way. I'll let you guys say why. I feel like we had one taken away from us."

The NFL promised to take a look at the tuck rule after the season and did, but no changes were made.

Again, any changes would have come too late to help the Raiders.

"It's my opinion, and just about everybody else's in the world, that it was a fumble," Al Davis said. "That they could reverse it without indisputable evidence is unbelievable."

And, unlike the Immaculate Reception, he didn't say it was an honest mistake.

Winning
the Big One

In the late 1960s and early 1970s, the road to the Super Bowl often ran through Oakland. Or, to be more precise, it often ran over the Oakland Raiders.

After the Raiders lost to the Green Bay Packers, 35–14, in Super Bowl II following the 1967 season, quarterback Daryle Lamonica told reporters in the locker room at the Orange Bowl in Miami, "We have a young team and we'll be back."

Although Oakland would win eight division titles in the next nine seasons and play in six American Football League or American Football Conference championship games, the Raiders would not make it back to the Super Bowl for nine years.

Counting 1967, the team that defeated the Raiders in the playoffs would win the Super Bowl seven times in nine seasons.

It all started when the Raiders lost the 1968 AFL Championship Game in the closing minutes to the New York Jets, 27–23. The Jets went on to make history when Joe Namath guaranteed victory over the Baltimore Colts in Super Bowl III and delivered, 16–7.

The following year, the Raiders beat Kansas City twice during the regular season, but Lamonica hit his hand on the helmet of defensive end Aaron Brown while following through on a pass early in the last AFL Championship Game.

Lamonica, unable to grip the ball properly, was ineffective and the Chiefs won, 17–7, before dismantling the Minnesota Vikings in Super Bowl IV, 23–7.

George Blanda rallied the Raiders in the first AFC Championship Game in 1970 at Baltimore, but the great Johnny Unitas threw a 68-yard touchdown pass to Ray Perkins to clinch the Colts' 27–17 victory. Baltimore beat Dallas in the Super Bowl, 16–13.

The Raiders missed the playoffs for the only time during that stretch in 1971, and the following year were knocked out in the first round by Franco Harris's Immaculate Reception in Pittsburgh.

Oakland eliminated Pittsburgh, 33–14, in the first round in 1973, but lost to Miami, 27–10, and the Dolphins beat Minnesota in Super Bowl VIII, 24–7.

The Raiders ended Miami's two-year run as Super Bowl champions on Clarence Davis's "Sea of Hands" catch in the 1974 playoffs, but Harris ran for a go-ahead touchdown on the first play of the fourth quarter and the Steelers won the AFC title at Oakland, 24–13. Pittsburgh went on to win its first world title, 16–6, over Minnesota.

Blanda completed a long pass to Cliff Branch on the last play of the 1975 AFC title game, but the Raiders ran out of time at the 15 yard line in icy Pittsburgh. The Steelers won, 16–10, and beat Dallas, 21–17, for a second consecutive Super Bowl title.

"We thought we'd be back every year," said Gene Upshaw, the Hall of Fame guard. "I was a rookie in '67 and we lost only one game before the Super Bowl, so I thought it was going to be easy to get back there.

"But we kept losing in the playoffs and they said we couldn't win the big one. I guess we couldn't because we didn't. It was frustrating because we were close so many times, and the team that would beat us would win the Super Bowl."

In 1976, that all changed.

The Raiders, despite a string of early season injuries to its defensive line, shook off a 48–17 loss at New England in week four and put together a 13–1 record.

Oakland needed a fourth-quarter rally to overcome the Patriots in the first round, 24–21, and dominated Pittsburgh in the AFC Championship Game, 24–7.

After that game, Upshaw met Mean Joe Greene under the stands in the Oakland Coliseum for something that amounted to a changing of the guard.

Kenny Stabler's touchdown run beats the Patriots, sending the Raiders to Super Bowl XI.

"He congratulated me and said that winning that game wasn't enough, that we had to keep up the AFC's superiority in the Super Bowl," Upshaw said. "And he told me that we wanted to play Minnesota, but I wasn't so sure.

"The Vikings had already lost three Super Bowls and I figured they had to beat somebody, I just didn't want it to be us. It was the law of averages. Once we got there, I found out what [Greene] meant."

But to reach the Super Bowl, the Raiders would have to survive a season that began in adversity when starting defensive linemen Horace Jones, Tony Cline, and Art Thoms were injured and knocked out for the season.

Coach John Madden was somehow able to turn that negative into positive energy.

"That gave us a sense of urgency right off the bat," Madden said. "We were so good that we knew we were always going to be there at the end of the season, but that year, with all the injuries we didn't know at the start what was going to happen.

"We didn't know what was going to happen with our defense, so there was no complacency. We got that sense of urgency early and we never lost it."

To make up for the sudden shortage of defensive linemen, the Raiders did two things that turned their season in the right direction. They brought in help from the outside, and they switched from the traditional 4–3 defense, with four down linemen and three linebackers, to a 3–4, or Orange defense in Raider terminology. What seemed to be an act of desperation turned out to be a stroke of genius.

Oakland had drafted 6'9", 285-pound Charles Philyaw out of Texas Southern. Philyaw was inserted at left end, and Oakland acquired 6'7", 270-pound Dave Rowe from the San Diego Chargers and made him the middle guard.

Although he wasn't immediately put into the lineup, the Raiders also signed 6'8", 275-pound John Matuszak, who had been the number one selection in the NFL draft by Houston five years earlier but now was out of football because of problems on and off the field.

John Matuszak

John Matuszak came to the Oakland Raiders in 1967 with a reputation as a party animal. He lived up to it.

"Cruisin' with the Tooz" was the term teammates used for a night out with Matuszak, a 6'8", 275-pound defensive end.

"Tooz Day" night was the evening Matuszak set aside for extended "cruisin' " because it was early in game week, although that didn't stop him from going out on any other night.

John Matuszak solidified the Raider defense in 1976.

Early in Super Bowl week at New Orleans at the end of the 1980 season, Matuszak announced that he would not be partying in the French Quarter that week, but instead would be prowling the bars to keep his teammates out of trouble.

Matuszak's policeman routine paid off.

A couple nights before the game, Matuszak rescued wide receiver Cliff Branch from some trouble with a few rednecks in a New Orleans bar.

On Super Bowl Sunday, Branch caught two touchdown passes in a 27–10 victory over the Philadelphia Eagles.

The Raiders had been a team that relied on its powerful offense while employing a quick, opportunistic defense, with linemen who were agile rather than exceptionally large. Suddenly, Oakland was mammoth up front and soon the defense would be dominating opponents.

Otis Sistrunk, the right end, had been the Raiders' largest starting defensive lineman at 6'4" and 270 pounds. Now he was the smallest.

But it wasn't as easy as it might sound.

"It was a complicated adjustment, the one we had to make," said linebacker coach Don Shinnick, who had played for the great Baltimore Colt teams of the late 1950s and early 1960s. "We had always used the 3–4 defense in specific situations. When we switched to it full time, we had to make it work for practically every situation we would face all year.

"That means twice as much teaching and twice as much learning. Just look at the basic numbers. A 4–3 means four men are rushing, three are playing linebacker, and four are in the secondary. Easy. In the 3–4, it is never that simple because there is always movement."

Going to the 3–4 also meant the Raiders had to find another starting linebacker and that turned out to be the best move Madden made.

He chose 6'2", 225-pound Willie Hall, who had played at USC and been cut by the Raiders the year before when they signed free agent linebacker Ted Hendricks, formerly of the Baltimore Colts, who was in the midst of a career that would take him to the Hall of Fame.

The Raiders would reap immediate dividends from going to the 3–4 and inserting Hall, but the big payoff would come during the playoffs.

"Not only did we get big up front when we went to the 3–4, but we got another great athlete on the field," said safety Jack Tatum, the Raiders' enforcer, who was the hardest hitter in football at the time.

"Willie Hall was a great athlete who made great plays. It seemed like he made at least one in every game. When we played a four-man line, we had no place for him."

Said Madden: "We didn't have a fourth defensive lineman who was as good as Willie Hall."

Hall fit perfectly into the Raiders' linebacking corps in the middle next to 6'5", 250-pound Monte Johnson. Outside were the 6'7", 225-pound Hendricks and Phil Villapiano, who at 6'2", 225 pounds was the hardest hitter of the group.

The Raiders covered receivers man to man with their splendid secondary of cornerbacks Willie Brown, another future member of the Hall of Fame who practically invented bump-and-run pass coverage, and Skip Thomas, with Tatum and underrated George Atkinson at safety.

It looked good on paper, but the first venture of the 3–4 defense was something of a disaster.

Oakland drew the two-time defending Super Bowl champion Steelers in the opener and fell behind, 28–14, with 6:43 left in the game at the Oakland Coliseum.

"I think we had the feeling that if we could only come back and almost catch them it would give us a boost," said wide receiver Fred Biletnikoff, yet another future Hall of Famer.

The Raiders tried to mount a comeback, but Kenny Stabler's pass was intercepted and Pittsburgh seemed headed for an insurance touchdown.

Just then, the 3–4 defense arrived.

Thomas forced Franco Harris to fumble and Johnson recovered at the Oakland 25. Stabler marched the Raiders to a touchdown in seven plays, hitting tight end Dave Casper with a 10-yard scoring pass and it was 28–21 with 2:56 left.

The Raiders forced the Steelers to punt, and special teams captain Warren Bankston, a former Steeler, partially blocked Bobby Walden's punt. Oakland had the ball on the Steelers' 29.

After three consecutive incomplete passes, Stabler found Cliff Branch for 27 yards to the 2. Then Stabler faked a pass to Casper and bootlegged left behind Upshaw for a touchdown to tie the score with 1:05 remaining, using a play the Raiders would use to save their season in the playoffs two months later.

The Steelers did not settle for overtime. Terry Bradshaw's pass was tipped by Rowe and intercepted by Hall on the Steelers' 13 yard line with a minute left. After two runs by Pete Banaszak, rookie Fred Steinfort, who had beaten out George Blanda during training camp, kicked the game-winning field goal from 21 yards with eighteen seconds left.

"It was a fun game," Stabler said afterward.

The fun would continue even though there were a few more potholes to negotiate along the way.

Although the Steelers had controlled much of the game, the Raiders had learned in the closing minutes in a trial by fire that their new defense could work when it counted most.

"We didn't play bad, we just kept breaking down," Tatum said. "When they got that big lead, we had only one aim left—get the ball for our offense.

"We learned something in that game. If we just worked harder than the other team, we could play defense as good as anybody in the league. We all had that feeling and it got us going."

If the Raiders needed any more incentive, they got it from Coach Chuck Noll of the Steelers, who after the game labeled Tatum and Atkinson "the NFL's criminal element."

They received another jolt a few weeks later in practice when Stabler took a bad step in practice and strained one of his fragile knees, which were a problem through much of his career.

Mike Rae, who had been most valuable player of the Rose Bowl while at USC before playing in the Canadian Football League, replaced Stabler in Houston and threw two touchdown passes to Branch to beat the Oilers, 14–13.

"That was pretty exciting," Rae said. "I had gone through a tough training camp just trying to make the team and then all of a sudden in the third game, there I am starting.

"We had such a tremendous supporting cast. That was such a great offensive line and the receivers we had, they made it a lot easier. One we got going, I settled down. I know John Madden played it conservatively that game, trying to make it easier for me. I hit Cliff on a down-and-out for the winning touchdown, and the defense saved us a couple of times."

The Raiders twice reverted to their 4–3 defense, inserting Matuszak when Houston had the ball inside the Oakland 5 yard line. On Houston's first possession of the game, "Tooz" threw Joe Dawkins for a loss of 3 yards to force a field goal.

Late in the third quarter, with the Raiders protecting a 7–6 lead, Dan Pastorini tried a quarterback sneak on fourth down from the 1 yard line and was thrown back by Tatum and Johnson.

"They just beat the heck out of us inside the 5," said Coach Bum Phillips of the Oilers. "When they line up all of their big linemen like that, we can't move a single inch. I'm impressed. Philyaw is bigger than the Shamrock Hilton."

Philyaw, whose college coach at Texas Southern said he didn't think he could make it in pro football, had his best game as a pro. He made seven tackles, including two sacks, and knocked down four passes. The hard part was getting him to the stadium.

He was summoned by a judge the night before the game because of an outstanding warrant from his college days. Jim Otto, now the Raiders' business manager, paid the fine and Philyaw was set free.

"If I'd known he was going to cause so much trouble against the Oilers, I never would have let him off," the judge said later.

He never made it as big as the Raiders had hoped, but instead left his teammates with a seemingly endless supply of Philyaw stories.

Once, Philyaw, who was running late while trying to get back to training camp in Santa Rosa for a Sunday night team meeting after a Saturday exhibition game, ran out of gas on Highway 101.

The Raiders were walking into the meeting when Philyaw showed up with his new car on the back of a tow truck. When he explained that he didn't have money to pay for gas, someone asked the rookie how he paid for the tow truck.

"I used my MasterCard," he said with a smile, pulling the credit card out of his pocket.

Another time, Philyaw asked fullback Mark van Eeghen, "Hey, Van, why are you the only player on the team who has your first and last name on the back of your jersey?"

A week after the Houston game, Philyaw and the Raiders both went down hard in a 48–17 trouncing by the New England Patriots in Foxboro, Massachusetts.

Philyaw left the field on a gurney after suffering a severely sprained ankle in the second quarter. Matuszak replaced him, and although no one knew it at the time, the final piece of the Raider puzzle was in place.

Tooz, despite his great size and athletic ability, had failed in stints with Houston, Kansas City, and Washington. But it soon became apparent that he was the perfect defensive end in the 3–4, and the left side of the Raider defense was virtually impassable for the rest of the season.

"He made our defense whole," Madden said.

Although the Patriots dominated the game, the Raiders learned some things that would help when New England visited Oakland in the playoffs eleven weeks later.

With the Patriots shutting down Branch and Biletnikoff outside, Stabler discovered tight end Dave Casper, another Raider who was on his way to the Hall of Fame. Casper, in his first year as a starter, caught twelve passes for 225 yards.

"What I remember about that game is Snake threw two touchdown passes to Freddie [Biletnikoff] early in the game and they called me for holding both times," Upshaw said. "We should have been ahead, 14–0.

"They got a couple of turnovers and things just steamrolled from there. But they never really stopped us; we stopped ourselves. We knew we could have won that game had things been different at the start and that helped us when we played them later."

Upshaw, 6'5" and 260 pounds, was the emotional leader of that 1976 Raider line that NFL Films has called the greatest offensive line in the history of the NFL. He played alongside tackle Art Shell for fifteen years and they will be together forever in the Hall of Fame.

Center Dave Dalby replaced Jim Otto, another Hall of Famer, in 1975 and snapped the ball on virtually every play as the Raiders won Super Bowls XI, XV, and XVIII. Overshadowed on the right side because of the strength on the left were guard George Buehler and tackle John Vella.

"Mean Joe Greene of the Steelers paid Buehler the ultimate compliment, saying he was one of the toughest guys for him to play against and probably the cleanest," Shell said. "The guy didn't know what holding was."

Stabler said the 6'2", 270-pound Buehler had "the perfect build to be a guard. He's a Coke machine with a head."

Vella was embarrassed by defensive end L. C. Greenwood of the Steelers on one series early in his career, allowing Stabler to be sacked, being flagged for holding Greenwood, and jumping offside in one short sequence.

After that, he had some of his best games against Greenwood and the Steelers.

"John Vella was tough mentally and physically," Shell said. "He was a great pass blocker. Dalby was as tough as a nail. He wasn't a big guy but he built himself up to 265 pounds. He was so durable, he just wouldn't leave the field.

"Gene was the prototype guard: big, strong, fast. He could really run. He would tell the backs, 'I'm going to the flag. If you want to score, get on my butt.' And they would."

Upshaw wore number 63 and the running backs called him "Highway 63."

Shell was, quite simply, one of the greatest tackles to play the game. He played perhaps the best game ever by an offensive lineman in Super Bowl XI when he dominated Jim Marshall of the Minnesota Vikings, one of the best defensive ends in the game.

A basketball player in college, Shell had incredible footwork for a 6'5", 280-pounder.

"Those feet start to move and that big body moves," marveled Coach Don Shula of the Miami Dolphins. "You need a $5.00 cab ride to get around him."

The Raiders won their last ten games of the 1976 regular season, gaining momentum as the defense got stronger, but everyone knew that eventually it would be all about Pittsburgh.

They were reminded as the Raiders were about to play Cincinnati in the next-to-last game of the regular season at Oakland on *Monday Night Football*.

Oakland already had wrapped up the AFC West title. Cincinnati surprisingly held a one-game lead over Pittsburgh in the AFC Central and could knock the Steelers out of the playoffs by beating the Raiders.

A story filtered out of Pittsburgh during the week quoting cornerback Mel Blount and several other Steelers as saying that the Raiders didn't want to play Pittsburgh in the playoffs again and would "lie down" against the Bengals.

"This team doesn't know how to lie down," Upshaw said, and the Raiders went out and proved it.

Stabler threw four touchdown passes and the Raiders rushed for 228 yards to control the game from start to finish in a 35–20 victory.

Shell, in a preview of his Super Bowl performance against Marshall, kept defensive end Coy Bacon, who had twenty-two sacks that season, off Stabler.

"I think he touched him once," Shell said.

Said Madden: "Of all the games I ever coached, that was the most proud I've ever been of a team. That game wasn't just about us, it was about the NFL. If that's the way things were done in the NFL, if a team would lie down like they were saying, football was in big trouble.

"We had everything clinched and there was no reason to win except for the integrity of the game. That game was good for us and it was good for football."

It was also good that the Raiders had the home field throughout the playoffs. Even so, New England again gave them trouble in the first round.

The Patriots held a 21–10 lead in the fourth quarter, but Stabler led two scoring drives in the final ten minutes, skirting left end himself from a yard away with ten seconds left to provide the winning points in a 24–21 victory.

Upshaw again was out in front blocking cornerback Mike Haynes, a future Raider who would help win Super Bowl XVIII.

"I had done a good job on Cliff Branch in that first game, so they didn't test me much in the playoffs," Haynes said. "I had an injured hamstring that we did a good job of keeping secret or maybe I could have made a play on Stabler."

Said Upshaw: "I've talked with Mike Haynes about that play, and I told him he couldn't have made that play if he had three good legs."

Nothing was going to stop the Raiders this time, not even the Steelers, who had beaten Oakland in the last two AFC Championship Games—and three times in the playoffs in the previous four seasons.

Upshaw had a dream of a convincing Raider victory during the week before the game, and when he came to practice the next morning, he wrote "Big Win" on a blackboard.

His dream came true, 24–7, even though the Steelers claimed it would have been different had injured running backs Franco Harris and Rocky Bleier been able to play.

"Sure, Rocky and Franco would have helped them," Dave Rowe conceded. "But tell me where they would have run. There were no holes."

The Raiders did the running instead, penetrating Pittsburgh's famed "Steel Curtain" defense for 157 yards.

Willie Hall intercepted a pass by Terry Bradshaw and returned it 25 yards to the Pittsburgh 1 yard line, and Clarence Davis scored Oakland's first touchdown on the next play for a 10–0 lead.

The Raiders made it 17–7 only twenty-three seconds before halftime when Stabler hit Warren Bankston on a 4-yard touchdown pass, out of a three tight end formation, and the former high school quarterback heaved the ball into the upper deck.

"I only scored five touchdowns in my career, so I threw the ball into the stands every time, but that one was special," Bankston said. "I might have had four Super Bowl rings had I stayed with the Steelers, but I got one in Oakland, and I had a lot more fun here."

All that was left was for Stabler to throw a 5-yard touchdown to Banaszak, and the Raiders were on their way to the big one, Super Bowl XI, some 400 miles down Interstate 5 at the Rose Bowl in Pasadena.

Madden, always a nervous wreck on game day anyway, thought all the Raiders were onboard when he told the bus driver to leave a few minutes before the appointed time on Super Sunday.

He didn't know Biletnikoff—who turned out to be the game's most valuable player for taking three passes to the Minnesota goalmouth, if not into the end zone—and several other players were still at the hotel.

Clarence Davis (28), following Mark van Eeghen, gained 137 yards in Super Bowl XI.

The players took cabs to the Rose Bowl and were hiding out from Madden in the locker room, but an assistant told him what was going on.

"Tell them it was my fault," Madden said. "I'm not mad at them."

But Madden uncharacteristically felt all week that the Raiders were going to win, and convincingly, especially when Stabler led the Raiders through a near-perfect practice on Thursday. The only pass he threw that hit the ground was dropped.

Things didn't start well when Ray Guy had a punt blocked for the first time in his pro career, and Minnesota reached the Oakland 2 yard line. But Tatum knocked the ball loose from Brent McClanahan, and Willie Hall, around the ball again, recovered.

Davis, who rushed for 137 yards as Shell pitched his shutout against Marshall, ran 35 yards to get the Raiders out of trouble. Eventually, Errol Mann kicked a field goal to give the Raiders a 3–0 lead.

Madden was unhappy that the Raiders had failed to score a touchdown, but Stabler told him, "Don't worry about it. There's plenty more where that came from."

And there was. The Raiders had a 19–0 lead before the Vikings got on the scoreboard on Fran Tarkenton's pass to Sammie White, but an interception by Hall dented any hopes the Vikings had of a comeback.

Dave Casper catches a touchdown pass from Kenny Stabler in Super Bowl XI.

Stabler, calling the plays himself as most quarterbacks did in those days, clinically sliced up Minnesota's famed "Purple Gang" defense for 429 total yards.

Bill King, the Raiders' radio voice and a classical music buff, said at one point, "Jascha Heifetz never played a violin with more dexterity than Kenny Stabler is playing the Minnesota Vikings this afternoon at the Rose Bowl stadium in Pasadena."

Willie Brown put an exclamation point on the 32–14 victory and the season in the closing minutes by intercepting Tarkenton's pass and taking it 75 yards for a touchdown. His return remains a Super Bowl record.

"When you've been around as long as I have, you know in certain situations there are only so many things a quarterback can do," Brown said. "I just felt that play was coming, so I told Jack [Tatum] to watch my back and I went for it."

The Raiders tried to carry Madden off the field but dropped him after a short trip, but he was feeling no pain.

And so the American Football League franchise that wasn't supposed to be, nearly died in infancy, and then couldn't win the big one, finally sat atop the pro football world.

Madden, who had been through the Immaculate Reception and all the other Raider disappointments, had a message for his team afterward.

"John said this one they can never take away from us," Upshaw said. "He was right. This one is ours forever."

Miami Nice

When the Miami Dolphins sculpted the greatest season in National Football League history, posting a spotless 17–0 record in 1972, it's a good thing they didn't run into the Oakland Raiders.

And that's not just Raider bravado.

The Raiders seemed to have Miami's number in those days, especially in Oakland.

Don Shula, who coached the Dolphins to consecutive Super Bowl titles in 1972 and 1973, won more games than any coach in NFL history, but he never won a game in Oakland in five tries, two of them in the playoffs.

"They had a great team, with great players and a great coach, but it was just one of those things that they couldn't beat us in Oakland," said Raider Coach John Madden. "We had some great games against them. Maybe the Dolphins just brought out the best in us."

Two of those games took place with the Dolphins at the top of their game.

Miami won eighteen consecutive games before coming to the Bay Area to face the Raiders on September 23, 1973.

The game was moved to Memorial Stadium at the University of California, Berkeley, because the Oakland Athletics, on their way to the second of three consecutive World Series titles, were playing at the Oakland Coliseum.

George Blanda kicked four field goals and the Raiders ended Miami's streak with a memorable defensive effort, 12–7. The Raiders couldn't duplicate that game later in the season when they fell to the Dolphins, 27–10, in the American Football Conference Championship Game at Miami.

"What I remember about the Berkeley game was the crowd," said Al LoCasale, executive assistant for the Raiders. "People said Raider fans wouldn't go to Berkeley because of logistical problems, parking and traffic, all of that.

"There were 74,121 people in the stadium, which was a northern California record for a professional football game, and more watching up on 'Tightwad Hill.' And they were loud."

So was the Raider defense, which held the vaunted Miami offense to 195 yards, 31 of which came on a harmless draw play by Mercury Morris against a prevent defense as time ran out in the first half.

The Dolphins' rushing game ground to a halt, with Morris gaining 48 yards, Larry Csonka managing only 47, and Jim Kiick being held to 10 yards on seven carries.

Bob Griese completed only twelve of twenty-five passes for a paltry 90 yards, and the Raiders, particularly All-Pro cornerback Willie Brown and hard-hitting safety Jack Tatum, held the great Paul Warfield without a reception.

"Warfield was a great receiver and he really ran the slant pattern well," Brown said. "I told him early in the game, 'Don't go inside today because Tatum is acting real crazy. Something is wrong with him.'

"So the first time Warfield runs a slant, Tatum really hits him hard and he drops the ball. I said, 'I told you not to run in there.' He didn't run a slant the rest of the game. Everything he did was outside, so it wasn't that hard to stop him."

The Raiders changed their tendencies in that game and perhaps caught the Dolphins off guard.

Against most teams, Oakland played strictly man-to-man

defense in the secondary. But against the Dolphins, the Raiders threw in some zone coverage, and Griese had trouble finding open receivers.

"We had a good mix of man to man and a roll-up, two-deep zone in that game," Brown said. "Miami had great players like Warfield, Csonka, and Morris, so they could score a lot of points and could score at any time.

"It was exciting to be able to shut them down."

Middle linebacker Dan Conners had a terrific game for Oakland, forcing Csonka to fumble on Miami's first series, and safety George Atkinson recovered on the Oakland 45 yard line. Conners, who made four tackles and broke up two passes, also recovered a fumble.

Miami threatened to score twice, but Garo Yepremian missed field-goal attempts of 26 and 45 yards. Finally, Griese hit tight end Jim Mandich on a 28-yard touchdown pass with 1:07 left in the game.

"They wouldn't have scored at all but the officials made a bad call to keep that drive alive," LoCasale said.

The Dolphins had three timeouts left and forced the Raiders to punt. Ray Guy, who averaged 49 yards on six punts, boomed a kick to the end zone that prevented a long return and forced Miami to try to go 80 yards. Griese threw four incomplete passes, two deflected by linebacker Gerald Irons, who also was in on ten tackles, and Miami's streak was history.

"The score doesn't show it, but we dominated the game," Madden said. "We moved the ball and we controlled the game, keeping it away from their offense. We just couldn't get into the end zone. We had twelve points, and that was enough, but it easily could have been in the twenties.

"We really studied them and what they did when they

Willie Brown

Willie Brown, possibly the greatest cornerback who every played, was so good that at times he would go several games without a pass being thrown his way.

Brown, who wasn't even drafted out of Grambling in 1963, had nine pass interceptions in 1964—his first full season as a starting cornerback with the Denver Broncos—and had seven in 1967—his first year with the Oakland Raiders.

But despite being selected All-AFL or All-Pro seven times in twelve years with the Raiders, Brown had only fifty-four interceptions in sixteen regular seasons, or just over three per year.

In the playoffs, however, Brown had seventeen interceptions in seven games and returned three for touchdowns.

"When you get to the playoffs, you are playing against the best quarterbacks and the best receivers, and they are not afraid to throw the ball against anybody," Brown said. "In those games I always knew I would get my chances.

"I always felt, no matter who I was playing against, if they threw the ball on my side, only two things could happen. Either it would be incomplete or intercepted."

Those three playoff touchdowns came against Fran Tarkenton, Bob Griese, and Terry Bradshaw—all enshrined with Brown in the Pro Football Hall of Fame.

Brown helped the Raiders to a 21-14 playoff victory over the Miami Dolphins in 1970 when he intercepted Griese's pass and ran 50 yards for a touchdown.

The Raiders beat the Pittsburgh Steelers 33-14 in the 1973 playoffs when Brown picked off Bradshaw's pass and returned it 54 yards for a score.

And in Super Bowl XI, Brown stole Tarkenton's pass and set a Super Bowl record with a 75-yard touchdown return during the Raiders' 32-14 victory.

Brown knew each one was coming.

"Even great quarterbacks, there are only so many things they can do," Brown said. "You watch films and study them to see what their tendencies are, to see what they like to do and what they do well, and that narrows it down even more. Sometimes I felt like I knew what the quarterback was going to do even before he did."

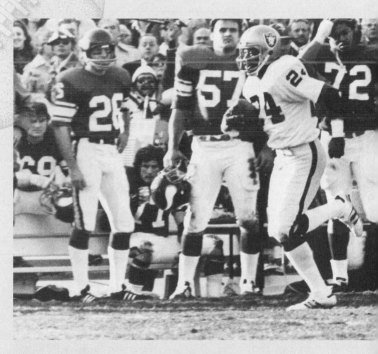

Willie Brown returns an interception 75 yards for a touchdown and a Super Bowl record. (Ron Riesterer/Oakland Tribune)

went 17–0. That was a great team, but we felt we really knew them well. We felt we could beat them and we did."

The Raiders also broke a tendency on offense. Daryle Lamonica completed seven of only ten passes for 63 yards as the Raiders went with a power running game. Fullback Marv Hubbard pounded out 88 yards, and halfback Charlie Smith added 80 of Oakland's 187 rushing yards.

Oakland reached Miami's 2, 3, and 12 yard lines, but each time the Dolphins stiffened.

Blanda kicked field goals of 12, 46, 19, and 10 yards (in those days the goalposts were on the goal line), one in each quarter.

"I didn't do much," Blanda said. "I just made the kicks I was supposed to make. We controlled the ball and our defense won the game."

The next time the Raiders beat Miami, it would be the offense's turn.

The Dolphins had won two consecutive Super Bowls and were trying to reach the NFL's ultimate game for the fourth year in succession when they came to Oakland four days before Christmas in 1974.

The Raider fans mimicked Miami's fans, who waved white hankies in games at the Orange Bowl stadium. Most of the 54,020 onlookers were waving black hankies as the teams took the field at the Oakland Coliseum.

"I've never heard more noise in that stadium than there was before the opening kickoff, not even since they expanded the seating capacity," LoCasale said. "It was so loud, I think the stadium lifted off the ground.

"Then, moments later, there was a deafening silence."

That's because Nat Moore of the Dolphins took the opening kickoff and returned it 89 yards for a touchdown without a

Raider laying a hand on him. After fifteen seconds, the Dolphins had a 7–0 lead.

"I remember the fans waving the hankies, everybody was so excited, and then right away we were behind," Madden said. "That really took the wind out of us, and it took us a while to get going."

But when the Raiders finally did get going, the Dolphins could not stop them in a game in which the lead changed hands seven times.

Miami held a 10–7 lead at halftime on Yepremian's 33-yard field goal with 1:01 left in the second quarter; then the second half was almost nonstop excitement.

The Raiders, who had not crossed midfield until midway through the second quarter, took their first lead on Kenny Stabler's touchdown pass to Fred Biletnikoff, but Oakland had to do it twice before it counted.

Stabler lofted a 40-yard pass that Biletnikoff caught in the right corner of the end zone despite skin-tight coverage by Tim Foley, but the official on the spot ruled Biletnikoff did not have both feet in bounds.

Several plays later, Stabler went back to Biletnikoff in the same corner, and this time Freddie made an incredible one-handed catch for a 13-yard touchdown. He had to catch the ball with one hand because Foley was holding the other one behind Biletnikoff's back.

Oakland had a 14–13 lead with 8:05 left in the third quarter, but Miami struck back eighty-seven seconds later when Griese hit Warfield for a 16-yard touchdown after linebacker Phil Villapiano was flagged for pass interference on a deep pass to Kiick.

Bubba Smith blocked the extra point, but Yepremian tacked on a 46-yard field goal and the Dolphins held a 19–14 lead with 11:50 left in the game.

The Raiders couldn't move the ball on their next possession and the Dolphins took five and a half precious minutes off the clock before being forced to punt.

The last five minutes sent the crowd into cardiac arrest.

Stabler threw long down the left sideline for Cliff Branch, who cut underneath cornerback Henry Stuckey and made a sprawling catch at the Miami 27 yard line. When Stuckey, who had replaced injured Curtis Johnson in the first quarter, over-

Kenny Stabler drove the Raiders the length of the field to dethrone Miami.

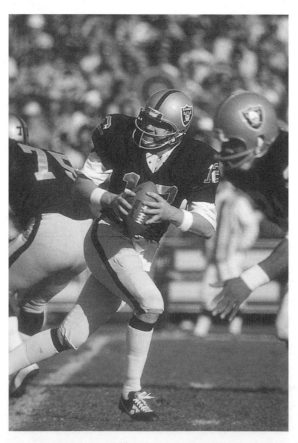

ran the play, Branch scrambled to his feet. Safety Charlie Babb came over to help, but Branch ran past him to complete a 72-yard touchdown.

"I was aware of Stuckey all the way," Branch said. "He was playing about 15 yards out, but I got a step on him. Kenny threw it a little short, so I turned and came back for it. Stuckey didn't turn until it was too late. Then I think he relaxed a little bit."

The Raiders had a 21–19 lead, but the crowd was anything but relaxed, especially when the Dolphins responded again like the champions they were with a 78-yard touchdown drive in only four plays.

Rookie running back Benny Malone swept right end and broke five tackles on a 23-yard touchdown run that gave Miami a 26–21 lead with 2:08 left in the game.

"I just wish Benny had fallen down at about the 3 yard line instead of going the full 23 yards for our last touchdown," Griese said later. "Benny made a beautiful run, but if he had stopped just short of the goal, we could have eaten up another minute and probably scored with less than a minute to go."

Stabler was one of the best at the two-minute drill and he had three timeouts to work with.

The Snake went right to his task, hitting Biletnikoff with passes of 18 and 20 yards over the middle, and the Raiders reached the Miami 43 yard line with 1:23 remaining.

"Everyone remembers how the game ended, but the thing was, we had to drive the length of the field against that great defense," Madden said. "They played that great deep zone, but they might have gotten a little soft in the middle.

"Stabler was able to get the ball inside to Fred, and we were able to move down the field pretty quickly. It was just a memorable drive."

Biletnikoff caught eight passes for 122 yards in the game, but Stabler would have to do the rest without him because the Dolphins threw a blanket over the Raiders' go-to receiver the rest of the way.

After two short completions and a 6-yard run by Clarence Davis, the Raiders had a first down on the Miami 14 yard line. Stabler called his last time-out with thirty-five seconds left.

After discussing the upcoming play with Madden, Stabler lingered on the sideline for a moment and gazed up into the stands.

"These fans sure are getting their money's worth today," the unflappable Stabler said.

(Merv Corning, the noted sports artist, credits the inspiration for his painting *Two-Minute Warning* to Madden's conferences with Stabler during the final minutes of this game.)

On the next play Stabler looked for Biletnikoff in the right corner, but he was covered. He also had Branch, tight end Bob Moore, and fullback Marv Hubbard running patterns that would reach the end zone.

But Stabler didn't have a chance to look for them because defensive end Vern Den Herder had broken away from tackle John Vella and was bearing down on the quarterback. Stabler tried to roll away to the left, and as Den Herder was pulling him down, he lofted a pass toward a black-shirted Raider in the left corner of the end zone.

It was Clarence Davis, who had the worst hands of any of the Raiders' backs and receivers and was surrounded by three Dolphins: Babb, Mike Kolen, and Larry Ball.

Somehow, Davis caught the ball—and bedlam ensued.

Defensive tackle Manny Fernandez sprinted to the end zone and tried to pry the ball from Davis' hands. The Raiders

Clarence Davis's "Sea of Hands" touchdown ends the reign of the Miami Dolphins.

poured onto the field in premature celebration and were penalized for unsportsmanlike conduct.

But Oakland held a 28–26 lead with twenty-six seconds left.

"[Den Herder] forced me out of the pocket and I started to run, and he dived at my legs and tripped me up," Stabler said. "In the course of falling down, I threw this end-over-end dying duck back into the corner of the end zone.

"Basically, I saw a black jersey there somewhere. I didn't even know who it was. I never should have thrown it. It was a dumb throw, but Clarence made a great catch. The ball probably should have been intercepted, but Clarence wanted it worse than they did.

"If it had been intercepted, I would be kicking myself for not throwing it away."

Said Davis: "When I saw the ball, I just concentrated. We [he and Kolen] got our arms on it at the same time, but the angel of mercy was riding on the ball. It was pure concentration.

"I was a secondary receiver, and when I knew the ball was coming to me, I was just hoping I could get it without somebody deflecting it. I was only supposed to be clearing out the area. I left my pattern when I looked back and saw Kenny scramble."

Miami still had some time left and got close to midfield, but Villapiano intercepted Griese's pass and the Dolphins' dynasty was history.

They seemed to know it.

"I think we had the best football dynasty ever," said Csonka, who played his last game for Miami that day, along with Kiick and Warfield, all three jumping to Toronto of the World Football League the next year. "They'll be chasing this one for a long time."

Said Shula: "This has to be the toughest loss I've ever suffered in coaching. When you lose that way, you know it wasn't meant to be. The season was meant to end here in Oakland and it did. The Raiders needed touchdowns to win and they got them."

Up in the NBC television booth, veteran commentator Al Derogatis told a national audience that it was "the greatest game I've ever seen."

Unfortunately for the Raiders and their fans, they couldn't summon the same emotion or performance the next week at the Coliseum and lost to the Pittsburgh Steelers in the AFC Championship Game, 24–13. The Steelers went on to beat Minnesota for the first of their first four Super Bowl victories.

That gave the Raiders another dynasty to deal with.

Holy Roller and Holy Toledos

Since the Oakland Raiders pulled off their first memorable rally to defeat the San Diego Chargers in 1963, the Silver and Black have become known for their epic comeback victories and fantastic finishes.

Some of the plays and games are among the most famous in NFL history and have catchy names such as the "Holy Roller" and "Ghost to the Post" or the "Heidi Game" and the "Sea of Hands Catch," while others are remembered mostly by the Raiders who pulled them off and the fans who watched them.

All were guaranteed to elicit a "Holy Toledo," the trademark call of Bill King, who described most of them on the Raider Radio Network.

The most controversial easily was the "Holy Roller," which took place at San Diego's Jack Murphy Stadium, perhaps the only stadium ever named after a sportswriter, on September 21, 1978.

The Chargers, who had become a long-time patsy of the Raiders after being an AFL powerhouse in the early years, held a 20–7 lead with 12:42 left in the game, but Kenny Stabler threw a 44-yard touchdown pass to Morris Bradshaw to get the Raiders back into the game.

It never should have happened, according to Coach John Madden of the Raiders.

"We played lousy," Madden said. "I was really mad at our team. We stunk. We never should have been in position to win the game."

Oakland got the ball back on its 20 yard line with 1:07 left, and Stabler, who had thrown three interceptions in the game, suddenly regained his touch and drove the Raiders down the field.

Stabler hit Bradshaw for 12 yards, Pete Banaszak for 14, Raymond Chester for 27, and Fred Biletnikoff for 13 to put the ball on the San Diego 14 yard line with sixteen seconds left before throwing a pass to Biletnikoff that fell incomplete in the end zone.

On second down, with ten seconds remaining, Stabler was pressured and grabbed by linebacker Woodrow Lowe. Before Lowe could take him down, Stabler flipped the ball forward with an underhanded motion, which the officials did not see.

"We had no time-outs and if I get sacked the game's over," Stabler said. "In a situation like that, you just fling the ball and hope something happens to it. I know damn well I fumbled.

"[Lowe] grabbed me and I was trying to throw the ball about the time I was hit. I fumbled it on purpose. Yes, I was trying to fumble. Hey, the breaks evened out. They got one of their touchdowns on a fluke."

The ball bounced past several Chargers toward the goal line. Banaszak, who missed his block on Lowe, reached it first on about the 12 yard line and got both hands on the ball as he was being taken down by a Charger, so he also flipped the ball forward.

"I knew what the situation was," Banaszak said. "I knew we were out of time-outs. If I fall on it, the game's over. I just bat-

Pete Banaszak (40) knocks the ball forward so Dave Casper (87) can recover to beat San Diego on "Holy Roller." (Ron Riesterer/Oakland Tribune)

ted it. I know it sounds like a fairy tale but the big guy upstairs was there, he gave us a break."

The ball bounced crazily toward the goal line and no one touched it until tight end Dave Casper of the Raiders caught up with the ball at about the 2 yard line. Casper tried to pick up the ball but couldn't get the handle. Then he used his feet like a soccer player and propelled the ball across the goal line before falling on it in the end zone.

"I tried to pick it up first and then I saw the fat line [goal line] go by so I fell on it," said Casper, a graduate of Notre Dame. "It was on the 3 when I saw it, and I made sure it went into the end zone. Notre Dame lost this week and God must have taken a vacation and come out here.

"[It] would've been nicer to do it a little smoother, with a little more skill and like a dancer or something. But I didn't, I did it like a klutz."

Pandemonium reigned.

"Madden is on the field," Bill King said on the Raider Radio Network. "He wants to know if it counts. The referee [Jerry Markbreit] says it does and get your big butt out of here. Madden does."

Markbreit's crew conferred briefly but called it a touchdown. There was no time left. Errol Mann kicked the extra point and the Raiders won, 21–20.

San Diego was stunned.

Ted Giannoulas, the man in the San Diego Chicken outfit, did a thirty-second collapse in the end zone seats.

"It was surreal," Giannoulas said. "It was absolute lunacy. No one knew at first if it was going to count or if it was a Charger victory. It was outright Raider thievery and cheating."

The Raiders didn't stick around for the fallout, running quickly to the locker room.

After the 1978 season, the NFL rules committee changed its rules concerning fumbles. On fourth down, or on any down inside the last two minutes of either half, only the fumbling player can recover the ball for a gain. If anyone else on the fumbling team recovers, the ball is returned to the spot of the fumble. But that didn't help the Chargers and their fans, who are still bitter about the play.

"We got raped," quarterback Dan Fouts said. "The official should have been ready for that play. Stabler couldn't afford to take a sack. He did the only thing he could do, he grounded the ball.

"If that were me, I suppose they would have penalized me for unsportsmanlike conduct. It still blows my mind."

Said Charger safety Glen Edwards: "The Raiders are the luckiest team in football."

When Casper was voted into the Hall of Fame in 2002, the play again became a topic of conversation. Although Casper had a great career as one of the best receiving and blocking tight ends ever, the "Holy Roller" surely helped him get to Canton, Ohio.

"If everybody would just have kept their mouths shut, instead of taking credit for it, they probably would've never made a big deal out of it," Casper said.

"But then, a couple days later, everybody's bragging, 'Well I knew I had to do this and I knew I had to do that,' so then they made a big stink and they changed the rules, which was the best thing that ever happened to me because they keep playing the darned play."

Casper and Stabler also were the principals in another famous play, "Ghost to the Post." The name is a little misleading because "Ghost," as Casper is known, did not go to the post as he was supposed to do.

The Raiders were locked in a bitter playoff struggle with the Baltimore Colts on Christmas Eve, 1977, at Memorial Stadium in Baltimore.

Stabler dueled with quarterback Bert Jones of the Colts. The lead changed hands or the score was tied on ten of the eleven scoring plays that day.

Ron Lee's second touchdown run of the game gave the Colts a 31–28 lead in the closing minutes.

The Raiders had one final chance in regulation. They faced third down and long from their 44 yard line when Stabler called a play on which Casper was supposed to run a post pattern.

Casper had been running crossing patterns and short curls all day against Baltimore's deep zone defense, but Stabler hoped he could find a crease and get open deep. As the play developed, Casper realized he couldn't run a post pattern and get open, so he improvised, because safety Bruce Laird, who earlier intercepted a pass by Stabler and returned it 61 yards for a touchdown, was waiting for Casper in the center of the field. So Casper started toward the post, but veered toward the right corner instead. Stabler read this change of direction on the fly.

Stabler's pass seemed uncatchable when he threw it, but it was thrown where only Casper could catch it, and he did, for a 42-yard gain to the Baltimore 14.

"If it looked tough, it really wasn't," Casper said of the catch. "I just ran under it and it stuck in my hands."

Casper looked back over his left shoulder initially, but the ball was thrown over his other one. He had to turn his head almost completely to the right during his adjustment to make the catch.

"I read Dave's move to the outside," Stabler said. "The safety was coming over, so I threw the ball to a spot where only

Casper could catch it. Maybe it wasn't a great throw, but it sure was a great catch."

The Raiders couldn't put the ball into the end zone but tied the score on Errol Mann's field goal with twenty-nine seconds left in regulation.

Stabler and Casper combined for their third touchdown pass of the game, a 10-yarder, forty-three seconds into the second overtime, ending the longest day in Raider history with a 37–31 victory.

When Casper was elected to the Pro Football Hall of Fame in 2002, he said the "Holy Roller" and "Ghost to the Post" deserved much of the credit.

Dave Casper (87) beat the Baltimore Colts with a touchdown catch in the second overtime.

"It's great to be known for those plays because people never forget them," Casper said. "They keep replaying them [on television] and I keep coming back."

Just like the Raiders, whose tradition of incredible comebacks and fantastic finishes began in 1963 when Al Davis came to Oakland and made a previously ragtag team believe it could win.

In a memorable but now nearly forgotten game on December 6, 1964, the Raiders were trailing the Buffalo Bills, 13–10, in the final minutes at Frank Youell Field in Oakland. Quarterback Tom Flores drove the Raiders downfield against the best defense in the American Football League, which led Buffalo to a 12–2 record that season and the first of two consecutive AFL championships.

The Raiders reached the Buffalo 1 yard line with one second left in the game. Flores called a time-out and went to the sideline to talk things over with Davis. During the time-out an incredible thing happened. Many of the 18,134 fans at tiny Youell Field came out of the stands and surrounded the twenty-two players on the field, leaving only enough room for the teams to run one last play.

It was the final hole of the British Open golf tournament coming to American football.

"It was amazing," said running back Clem Daniels of the Raiders. "The fans were so close at Frank Youell Field anyway, and there were really no barricades to keep them off the field. They were all around us.

"Everyone thought we were going to run the ball, but we faked an off-tackle trap. I hit the line and kept going, trying to make the Bills think I had the ball."

But the play Flores and Davis had decided to call was a pass to brilliant wide receiver Art Powell, who was working against cornerback Butch Byrd, one of the best in the AFL.

It was do or die.

"Art was a big guy, about 6'3", so he had a height advantage and he had great hands, but Byrd was very physical," Flores said. "It was a classic matchup. The play was a quick out. They were too tough against the run, so it had to be a pass. I threw it hard and high."

Powell caught the ball, with Byrd hanging on him like a cheap suit, for the winning touchdown. With the fans already on the field, it was instant bedlam. The delirious crowd mobbed Powell and eventually several fans lifted him onto their shoulders and carried him around the field for about fifteen minutes.

Flores headed for the locker room at the far end of the stadium—with a fan hanging on him almost the entire length of the field. Finally, the quarterback realized he knew the man.

"He was from my hometown, Sanger," Flores said. "My brother would bring a busload of people from Sanger to every home game. Frank Youell Field, that was a unique time and place. It will never happen again."

Daniels had a similar experience. At first he yelled at no one in particular, "Get off the field. We have to kick the extra point."

But soon, he too headed for the locker room, with a young fan attached to him all the way. Finally, he realized it was one of his students at Skyline High in Oakland, where Daniels was a physical education teacher, plus the golf and wrestling coach after the season.

"Frank Youell was an amazing little stadium," Daniels said. "We had some great days there. Everyone was involved because they were so close and the emotion was unbelievable. It took some adjusting when we moved into the Oakland

Coliseum, but it was a new era and it was necessary for the growth of the Raiders. But those who were there at Youell Field will never forget it."

Frank Youell Field is long gone and all that remains is a plaque on a light pole in a parking lot at Laney College commemorating the spot. But what magic the Raiders and their fans created there lives on.

The Raiders refined their comeback act at the Coliseum, especially when Kenny Stabler took over as the starting quarterback in 1973.

"Kenny Stabler was as good as any quarterback I've ever seen in the two-minute drill," Coach John Madden said.

Even before he became the starter, Stabler did it to the Pittsburgh Steelers in the 1972 playoffs with a 30-yard touchdown run with 1:13 left in the game before being upstaged by Franco Harris' Immaculate Reception.

Stabler did it to the New England Patriots in the 1976 AFC Championship Game; he did it to the Miami Dolphins on Clarence Davis's "Sea of Hands" catch in the 1974 playoffs; he did it to the Baltimore Colts on "Ghost to the Post" in the 1978 playoffs; and he did it to the San Diego Chargers on the "Holy Roller" in 1978. He did it to the Washington Redskins and Atlanta Falcons in consecutive overtime victories in 1975. He did it to the Steelers in the 1976 opener.

And on and on.

The Raiders were trailing the Cincinnati Bengals, 27–23, with fifty-five seconds left on October 20, 1974, when Stabler and the offense got the ball on the Oakland 40 yard line with no time-outs remaining.

The Bengals were double covering Cliff Branch and Fred Biletnikoff on the outside, so Stabler hit tight end Bob Moore down the middle for three big pass plays, then connected with number three wide receiver Mike Siani for 20 yards to the Cincinnati 2 yard line.

There were eight seconds left, so the Bengals braced for perhaps two Stabler throws into the end zone. Instead, Stabler handed the ball to Charlie Smith on a sweep, not knowing that Smith had injured a knee while pass blocking a few plays earlier. But the Bengals were so fooled that Smith was able to limp to the goal line and dive into the end zone with two seconds left, giving the Raiders a 30–27 victory.

"They were jamming our outside receivers so we couldn't complete a pass out there and get out of bounds to stop the clock," Stabler said. "The middle was wide open, so we took advantage of it and used the clock well. Since we had connected with five straight passes moving down the field, we knew the Bengals would be all over our receivers on that last play with such little time left. We won because we went against our tendencies all the way down the field."

Said Smith: "I hyperextended my knee and couldn't cut or make any moves, but I thought I could run to the flag. I took the handoff and was a little wobbly, but Gene Upshaw was out in front of me and he blocked the only guy who had a chance to get me.

"Al Davis asked me, 'Why did you dive?' I told him I just wanted to make sure."

Stabler left the Raiders in 1980, but he had one last comeback in him when Oakland played at New Orleans on December 3, 1979.

Quarterback Archie Manning's two touchdown passes helped the Saints build a 28–7 lead in the second quarter. New Orleans led, 35–14, in the third quarter after Stabler's pass was tipped and intercepted by Ken Bordelon, who returned it 19 yards for a touchdown.

Training Camp

During the 1960s and 1970s, the Oakland Raiders spent eight weeks in training camp, more than any other team. They made the most of it, on and off the field.

"Players would get traded to other teams and they couldn't believe they were back in town in three or four weeks," said guard Gene Upshaw. "Guys would be traded to us and they couldn't believe how long our camps were.

"We would tell them, 'We're going to be here for a while.' "

Training camp for the Raiders was the El Rancho Motel on the outskirts of Santa Rosa, about 60 miles north of Oakland. Most pro football teams held their training camps on college campuses.

Two practice fields and a locker room were constructed behind the hotel, but aside from practice and meetings, it was a bit like grown-up kids at summer camp.

Linebacker Ted Hendricks once rode onto the practice field on a horse.

Another time, players paid a stripper from a topless bar down the street to streak the practice field.

Guard George Buehler would spend his free time building model cars and planes, including a tank that he could send by remote control to the Raider office to pick up his mail.

At least once during every camp, the hotel Jacuzzi would overflow with soapsuds. No one ever admitted to doing it, but trainer George Anderson was the prime suspect.

Camp was not official until Upshaw got into a fight on the field with defensive tackle Art Thoms.

"We built a lot of camaraderie in training camp, but after a while, it got old," Upshaw said. "It was eight weeks of two practices a day in pads. Going against the same guys all the time got old, and you got tired of certain things, so there would be fights. They didn't mean anything. When they were over, we forgot about them and would go have a drink."

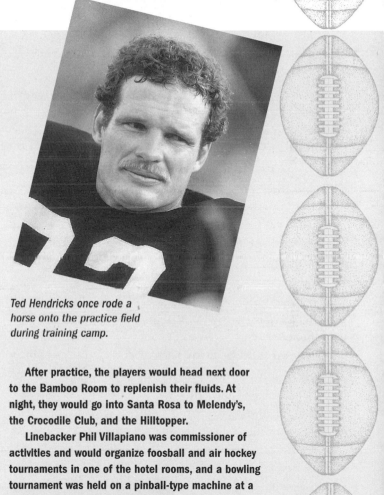

Ted Hendricks once rode a horse onto the practice field during training camp.

After practice, the players would head next door to the Bamboo Room to replenish their fluids. At night, they would go into Santa Rosa to Melendy's, the Crocodile Club, and the Hilltopper.

Linebacker Phil Villapiano was commissioner of activities and would organize foosball and air hockey tournaments in one of the hotel rooms, and a bowling tournament was held on a pinball-type machine at a bar down the street.

"If you're not cheating, you're not really trying," was the motto in these tournaments.

On the last week of camp, the players were given the night off for the annual "Rookie Party" at a bar in Santa Rosa.

Then the Raiders were ready to start the season.

Stabler, who had thrown an interception and lost a fumble to set up two earlier New Orleans touchdowns, was knocked woozy trying to make a tackle on Bordelon.

"Kenny got dinged pretty good," Coach Tom Flores said. "He didn't know where he was, but when I went to put Jim Plunkett in at quarterback, Stabler ran to the huddle and sent him off.

"I guess he figured he helped us get in the hole, so he wanted to make it up. I decided to leave him in for just one series. Then I decided to leave him in for another and another."

Stabler hit five passes on that first series, leading to Mark van Eeghen's 1-yard touchdown run, and later Stabler hit tight end Derrick Ramsey with a 17-yard touchdown pass to pull the Raiders to within 35–28.

With just over three minutes left, Stabler hit Cliff Branch with a pass on the left sideline that turned into a 66-yard touchdown to tie the score.

Then safety Mike Davis recovered a fumble by Chuck Muncie of the Saints and lateraled to linebacker Ted Hendricks, who took the ball to the New Orleans 13 yard line.

On third down from the 8 yard line, Stabler hit Branch for a touchdown with 1:54 left and the Raiders won, 42–35.

"I've never been in a game where I thought I was out of it," Stabler said. "We've had a lot of experience at [coming from behind to win]. We've been there before and we've been pretty successful."

The Raiders had two other memorable comebacks on *Monday Night Football*, rebounding from 24–0 deficits both times to win.

In their first home game at the Los Angeles Coliseum on November 22, 1982, after moving south from Oakland, the Raiders fell behind the powerful San Diego Chargers, 24–0, late in the second quarter. In 318 games since their inception in 1960, the Raiders had never rallied to win from a deficit that large.

But Muncie, now with the Chargers, fumbled and Hendricks recovered on the San Diego 17 yard line to set the comeback in motion. Jim Plunkett threw a 1-yard touchdown pass to Todd Christensen to get the Raiders on the scoreboard.

Marcus Allen had touchdown runs of 3 and 6 yards in the third quarter, and the Raiders were within three.

Plunkett engineered an 80-yard touchdown drive in the final quarter, with fullback Frank Hawkins going over from the 1 with 5:54 remaining. Rookie safety Vann McElroy intercepted a pass by Dan Fouts to help seal the victory.

"We've gained thousands of fans who have learned not to leave before the game is over," guard Mickey Marvin said. "With us, it often goes down to the wire. The Raiders have been doing this for a long time, way before I came here in 1977."

They did it again on Monday night in Denver on September 26, 1988, after the Broncos built a 24–0 lead at halftime, behind John Elway.

Quarterback Jay Schroeder hit fullback Steve Smith on short passes that turned into touchdowns of 40 and 42 yards in the third quarter, and the Raiders were within ten points.

After Chris Bahr kicked a 28-yard field goal early in the fourth quarter to inch the Raiders closer, Steve Strachan recovered a Denver fumble on the ensuing kickoff at the Denver 17 yard line. Then Marcus Allen ran 4 yards for a touchdown and the score was tied, 24–24, with 9:26 remaining.

Rich Karlis kicked a 25-yard field goal to give Denver the lead with 3:01 left, but Bahr matched it from 44 yards with eight seconds left and the game went to overtime.

Rookie Tim Brown of the Raiders returned a punt 74 yards for what looked like a game-winning touchdown, but the play was nullified by a penalty and they played on. Finally, safety Zeph Lee of the Raiders intercepted a pass by Elway to set up a 35-yard field goal by Bahr. The Raiders prevailed, 30–27, after seventy-two minutes and thirty-five seconds.

After more than forty years of this, Raider fans have learned not to despair when their team falls behind.

Quarterbacks Jeff Hostetler and Rich Gannon have continued the tradition in recent seasons.

"When you play the Raiders, you have to play for sixty minutes, because we never think we're beaten," Gene Upshaw once said.

In any era.

Wild Card Trumps

The Kenny Stabler Era ended in Oakland when the Raiders went 9–7 in 1979 and missed the playoffs for the second consecutive year.

Owner Al Davis went looking for another strong-armed quarterback to carry the Raiders into the 1980s, not realizing the next great Oakland quarterback was already on his roster.

Stabler never really fit into the mold of the quarterback Davis wanted to run his high-powered offense, except for one vital aspect: He was a winner. When he didn't win as much, he was gone.

"It was different without Snake because he had been our security blanket for so many years," said Tom Flores, who had taken over as coach of the Raiders when John Madden retired after the 1978 season. "But when it was time for Stabler to go, he had to go."

Flores knew from experience. He was the first quarterback of the Raiders in 1960 and led the team through its formative years before being traded to Buffalo in 1967 for Daryle Lamonica, who took Oakland to Super Bowl II in his first season.

The Raiders were hoping for a similar scenario when they sent Stabler to the Houston Oilers for younger, stronger Dan Pastorini—a northern California native who had been a star at Bellarmine High in San Jose and the University of Santa Clara.

Pastorini was installed as the starter ahead of Jim Plunkett, the former Heisman Trophy winner from Stanford, who had backed up Stabler for two years after signing with the Raiders when he was cut by the San Francisco 49ers.

"We told Jim that we traded a starter for a starter, so we had to start Pastorini," Flores said. "I remember Plunkett asked to be traded or released so he could have a chance to start somewhere else. Thank goodness we didn't do it, but I'm not sure I even took it to Al. We needed him.

"But to be honest, Jim deserved to be the starter. He played better than Pastorini in training camp and the preseason. In fact he probably deserved to be the starter the year before because he was playing better than Stabler."

Pastorini got off to a promising start when he threw two touchdown passes to newly acquired wide receiver Bob Chandler in a 27–14 victory at Kansas City, where the Raiders always had trouble winning, and Oakland won two of the first three games.

But the Raiders didn't score an offensive touchdown in a 24–7 setback at Buffalo, and Oakland's season seemed to be on the verge of disaster when Pastorini suffered a broken leg in a 31–17 loss to Kansas City at the Oakland Coliseum.

Few people saw the silver-and-black lining in the ominous clouds when Plunkett threw touchdown passes to Chandler and Cliff Branch in the fourth quarter against the Chiefs.

"I was upset when they didn't even give me an opportunity to compete for the job when they traded for Pastorini," said Plunkett, another northern California native who had played for James Lick High in San Jose and was now thirty-two years old.

"I was getting older and I was running out of time. You don't want anybody to get hurt, but when Pastorini broke his leg, it was an opportunity I sorely needed. I was physically and mentally ready."

Plunkett's body and psyche had been beaten and battered on mediocre teams with the 49ers and the New England Patriots, so few people expected him to get the Raiders back on track. But Plunkett reached into his youth to become the player and quiet leader everyone expected him to be when the Patriots made him the number one overall pick in the NFL draft, after he led Stanford to a big upset of Ohio State in the 1971 Rose Bowl.

"I was about as far down as you could be after I was released by San Francisco," Plunkett said. "I went from the number one pick to out of the league. I thought about quitting and getting into some other kind of business.

"But I knew I could still play."

Oh, could he.

Plunkett led the Raiders to six consecutive victories and had a 13–2 record as a starter that season, including four play-off victories, capped by a 27–10 rout of the Philadelphia Eagles in Super Bowl XV.

But after five games, the Raiders were 2–3 with a quarterback who had not played regularly for three years.

"We weren't playing badly, but we just had to play better and the players understood that," Flores said. "There were rumors that I was going to be fired and there was a lot of stress, but we never did panic.

"Nobody moped. We had enough leadership. Guys like Gene Upshaw, Art Shell, and Cliff Branch had been with us for a long time, and they helped hold things together."

Added tight end Raymond Chester: "We dug ourselves a hole and we had to get out of it. We had enough veterans that we knew we could pull together and get things going in the right direction.

"We had been around Jim Plunkett long enough to know that he had the ability, so we had confidence in him. John Madden used to say that when the ship started smoking, the rats would jump off. Well, we all stayed on."

The Raiders had lost to the San Diego Chargers, 30–24, in overtime in week two, but Kenny King ran 89 yards for a touchdown to break a tie in the fourth quarter and Oakland beat San Diego, 38–24, to start the winning streak.

Plunkett played well against the Chargers, but he really got it going in an electrifying 45–34 victory at Pittsburgh on *Monday Night Football*, cutting up the remnants of the legendary "Steel Curtain" defense for 247 yards and three touchdowns. There were nearly 800 yards of total offense and 258 yards on returns in the game, including a 34-yard fumble return for a touchdown by linebacker Rod Martin of the Raiders.

"Man, it was Pearl Harbor out there," said defensive end John Banaszak of the Steelers. "It was bombs away."

Said Flores: "Any time you beat the defending world champions on their field, it has to be a super win."

Next, Plunkett threw three touchdown passes in the second half to beat Seattle, 33–14, and two more the next week as the Raiders held off Miami, 16–10, to improve their record to 6–3.

The following week Plunkett ran 4 yards for a touchdown with 5:28 left to ensure a 28–17 victory over the Cincinnati Bengals. Later in the season, he would run 8 yards for a score to beat the Denver Broncos, 6–3.

"Jim was an ugly runner, but he was a good scrambler," Chester said. "He never got enough credit for that. He was good moving around in the pocket to buy time. We had a lot of tough guys on our team, but to me, he was the toughest."

Plunkett's toughness came into play against the Philadelphia Eagles, who ended the Raiders' streak at six with a 10–7 victory on Wilbert Montgomery's 3-yard touchdown run with 2:56 left. The Eagles, who won their eighth consecutive game, unleashed defensive end Claude Humphrey and an array of blitzes on Plunkett. He must have had flashbacks of his days in New England, because he absorbed eight sacks.

Still, Plunkett threw an 86-yard touchdown pass to Cliff Branch with 12:23 left to give the Raiders a 7–3 lead.

"Even though we lost, it was an advantage for us when we played them later," Plunkett said. "We made some changes in our pass protection and they didn't change much at all, maybe because they won. But it wasn't like they blew us out."

The Raiders won three of their last four games, losing to the Dallas Cowboys, 19–13, when Plunkett's pass into the end zone was intercepted by Aaron Mitchell with 1:44 left.

But Plunkett threw touchdown passes to Branch and Chester as the Raiders beat the New York Giants, 33–17, at East Rutherford, New Jersey, to clinch a wild card berth, making the playoffs for the first time in three years.

"It's sudden death from here on in," Upshaw, who had been through the playoff wars since 1967, told his teammates in the locker room at Giants Stadium. "You win, you go on. You lose, you go home."

What awaited the Raiders was an incredible four-game ride, in four distinctly different environments.

Up first would be the Houston Oilers, the preseason favorite to win the Super Bowl, who were quarterbacked by none other than Kenny Stabler. The Oilers also had former Oakland tight end Dave Casper and running back Earl Campbell.

But Stabler had to deal with Lester Hayes of the Raiders, who has having one of the best seasons a cornerback ever had. Hayes, who intercepted thirteen passes during the regular season, picked off two of Stabler's passes and also blitzed off the corner to sack his former teammate twice.

The Raiders greeted Stabler by sacking him seven times in all.

"They never did that when I was here," Stabler said of Hayes's corner blitzes.

The Oilers had a 7–3 lead on Campbell's 1-yard touchdown run in the first quarter, but the Raiders shut them out in the last three quarters of a 27–7 victory.

Oakland took a 10–7 lead on Plunkett's 1-yard touchdown pass to tight end Todd Christensen early in the second quarter and broke it open on Plunkett's 44-yard scoring pass to running back Arthur Whittington going down the right sideline on the first play of the fourth quarter.

Hayes, whose first interception against Stabler came in the end zone to snuff out a Houston threat, clinched the victory when he returned his second theft for a touchdown.

"I've been watching Snake since I first came into the league in 1977, and he throws the most beautiful 17-yard pass there is," said Hayes, who would finish the season with seventeen interceptions in twenty games. "I went into the game thinking if he tried one of those on my side, I would score."

Said Houston Coach Bum Phillips: "We were outplayed and outcoached. The Raiders played as well as any team I've seen in my twelve years of pro ball. Sack after sack built their momentum, and the harder they came."

The Raiders were underdogs the next week at Municipal Stadium in Cleveland, hard by the shores of icy Lake Erie. Flores knew the weather wouldn't bother his team, especially after practice the day before the game at Baldwin-Wallace College.

"We heard all week that we were going to die in the cold weather," Flores said. "But at practice on Saturday, our guys were throwing snowballs at each other, building snowmen, and rolling around in the snow. Our guys always were a little goofy.

"The Browns, who were the cold-weather team, worked out in a field house on Friday and didn't practice at all on Saturday. But I didn't know it was going to be as cold as it turned out to be on Sunday. When we got to the stadium, I could see that the lake was frozen."

That led to a decision by Flores that turned out to be a huge factor in the game.

The temperature hovered around zero, but it was minus thirty-seven with the wind-chill factor. Center Dave Dalby gave the Raiders the edge in the pregame psych-out when he went out on the field to talk to friends of his who played for the Browns. He was dressed in full football gear below the waist, but other than that wore only a T-shirt.

"The Browns thought he was nuts," Plunkett said.

Cleveland scored first when Ron Bolton picked off Plunkett's pass and ran 42 yards for a touchdown in the second quarter, but linebacker Ted Hendricks blocked the extra point.

The Raiders took a 7–6 lead when Mark van Eeghen powered in from a yard away with eighteen seconds left in the half after Plunkett hit Chester for 26 yards on third down and 13 yards to go.

"It was so cold I didn't want to leave the field at halftime," tackle Art Shell said. "I wanted to stay out on the field and play, because I was worried that once we went inside to get warm, I'd have a hard time coming back out. It was the coldest I've ever been."

At halftime Flores made his critical decision, deciding to defend the goal opposite the lake in the third quarter instead of taking the ball to start the second half. It gave the Browns an extra possession, but Flores trusted his defense.

"I wanted to defend the goal on the lake end in the fourth quarter," Flores said. "It was completely frozen on that end of the field. It was hard to do anything down there all day. I knew it was going to be close in the fourth quarter."

Not only would Cleveland have to deal with the icy end of the field, the Raiders would get the wind in the fourth quarter.

"There were only five passes completed into the wind all day," Plunkett said.

Don Cockroft, who had missed two field goal attempts into the wind at the icy end of the field in the first half, gave the Browns a 12–7 lead by kicking two 30-yard field goals in the third quarter.

In the fourth quarter, the Raiders rode the wind as Plunkett completed passes of 13 yards to van Eeghen, 19 to Branch, and 27 to Chester to set up van Eeghen's 1-yard touchdown run that gave Oakland a 14–12 lead with 9:22 left.

The Raiders drove again, but the Browns stopped them on fourth down when Flores passed up a chance for a field goal. Cleveland began its own drive behind quarterback Brian Sipe and reached the Oakland 13 yard line in the final minute.

Remembering Cockroft's earlier problems at that end of the field, Coach Sam Rutigliano passed up a field goal attempt and went for a touchdown. Sipe, pressured by the 6'7" Hendricks, passed for tight end Ozzie Newsome in the end zone, but strong safety Mike Davis cut in front and made a game-saving interception with forty-one seconds remaining.

"I don't know how Mike Davis ever caught that ball and I will never know," Flores said. "He had the worst hands. You could throw him the ball from 3 feet and he would drop it. When Clarence Davis caught the pass to beat Miami in 1974, they said he had bad hands, but Clarence had great hands

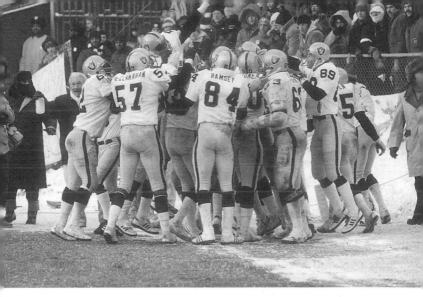

The Raiders mob Mike Davis after his interception sealed victory in icy Cleveland.

compared to Mike Davis. But Mike made the million-dollar catch."

The Raiders were still getting over the effects of the cold when they flew to San Diego, where it was eighty degrees, for the AFC Championship Game.

There they were prohibitive underdogs against the San Diego Chargers, who had prolific quarterback Dan Fouts and innovative coach Don Coryell, whose lethal passing game was known as "Air Coryell."

Few gave the Raiders a chance.

"When we got to San Diego on Friday night, the Chargers had already made their Super Bowl reservations for New Orleans," Art Shell said. "We might as well have not shown up. Then, on Saturday, Henry Lawrence suggested I remind our team what it takes to win a championship game.

"I told them what Joe Greene of the Steelers told me when we beat them for the AFC Championship in 1976 to get to Super Bowl XI: 'You do everything you can to win the big game. You scratch, you claw, you get it done.'

"Then on Sunday morning it rained and I took it as an omen that it was going to be our day because the Raiders always play well in bad weather."

The clouds cleared and it was a sunny—almost balmy day—in Bordertown.

The Chargers' theme song, "San Diego Super Chargers," blared from loudspeakers, and the "World Famous San Diego Chicken" entertained the crowd. It was a festive crowd, in the mood for a victory over the hated Raiders and a trip to the Super Bowl.

But it was a Raider day from the start when tight end Raymond Chester caught a deflected pass from Plunkett and outran the San Diego defense for a 65-yard touchdown 1:35 into the game.

"I was sick as a dog," said Chester, who had five receptions for 102 yards in the game. "I had a stomach problem. I didn't know

The Chargers couldn't stop Mark van Eeghen in the 1980 AFC Championship Game.

if it was an ulcer or what, but I couldn't sleep or keep anything down. I was concerned with how I was going to play.

"I had played eleven years to that point, and I don't remember having a ball that was tipped bounce right to me like that. Once I got the ball, it was just a footrace, and I always enjoyed footraces."

Chester, even though he was 6'4" and 240 pounds, had run the 100-yard dash in 9.7 seconds while at Morgan State. His touchdown ignited a twenty-one-point first quarter by the Raiders, and they increased the lead to 28–7 on van Eeghen's 3-yard scoring run in the second quarter.

They needed all of it.

"We couldn't play conservative with them," Flores said. "We knew this would be a game of big plays and touchdowns, with a lot of scoring, like the old AFL days. We had the lead, but the Chargers kept coming."

Fouts rallied the Chargers, who closed to within 28–24 late in the third quarter and then 34–27 with 6:43 left in the game, when the Raiders held San Diego inside the 10 yard line and forced a field goal by Rolf Benirschke.

On the sideline Flores told Plunkett the Raiders were not going to get conservative. They wanted to run the ball and use the clock, but they weren't afraid to throw the ball, if necessary, to get vital first downs.

As they were talking, the defense came off the field, and Hendricks told Plunkett, "We can't stop them. You can't let them get the ball back."

The Raiders didn't.

Whittington returned the kickoff to the Oakland 25 yard line and the Raiders pounded out 68 yards, many of them on punishing inside runs by van Eeghen, converting one third down after another.

"We're coming right at you," Upshaw was yelling at defensive tackles Gary "Big Hands" Johnson and Louie Kelcher on every play. "We're coming right in here again. You can't stop us."

The crowd was wild when the Raiders got the ball, but it soon fell silent. Many of the fans were gone by the time the clock ran out with Oakland inside San Diego's 10 yard line.

Fouts was cheering on his defense at the start, but soon he, too, gave up as Oakland's offensive line of Shell, Upshaw, Chester, Dalby, guard Mickey Marvin, and tackle Henry Lawrence took control of the game by killing the clock and the Chargers' chances.

"I saw Fouts on their sideline and he was pacing like a caged animal," Flores said. "He couldn't wait to get back into the game, but we never let him. After a while, I didn't see him any more. I think he went and sat down."

In Super Bowl XV, the Raiders again were underdogs.

NFL Films was so sure the Philadelphia Eagles would win, Coach Dick Vermeil was miked for sound on the field, as was assistant Dick Coury upstairs in the press box.

"Super Bowl Sunday," Lester Hayes said as NFL Films trained a camera on him during warm-ups. "And we're gonna win."

The Raiders gave their players cars during the week so they could enjoy the New Orleans nightlife, and led by John Matuszak, they were a presence on Bourbon Street all week. Matuszak broke curfew and was fined, but he said he was just watching out for his teammates.

Vermeil, who had the Eagles in team meetings at night, said any of his players who were caught out on the town would be sent home.

"It was the paramilitary team against the undisciplined team that was lucky to be there," Flores, whose Raiders became

Cliff Branch (21) takes the ball from Roynell Young for a Super Bowl XV touchdown.

the first wild card team to win the Super Bowl, said. "We gave the guys cars so they could go out and relax when they weren't practicing, in meetings, or dealing with the media. We weren't going to have curfew, but our guys asked to have one.

"You wouldn't believe the number of coaches who have thanked me for winning that game. Had they won, [Vermeil's] way would have been the wave of the future. Everybody would have had three-and-a-half-hour practices and endless meetings. On game day the disciplined team made all the mistakes."

It started less than two minutes into the game when linebacker Rod Martin made the first of his three interceptions against quarterback Ron Jaworski of the Eagles. That led to Plunkett's 2-yard touchdown pass to Cliff Branch and the Raiders were ahead for good.

Later in the first quarter, Plunkett scrambled and found running back Kenny King behind defensive back Herman

Rod Martin

As the Oakland Raiders prepared to make their first of two picks in the twelfth and final round of the 1977 National Football League draft, Coach John Madden scanned the list of available candidates.

He didn't like what he saw.

"There almost isn't anybody here who is worth the pick," he said. "There has to be somebody walking around the USC campus who is better than what's here."

So Madden got on the phone and called USC Coach John Robinson, his friend since childhood in Daly City, California, and running backs coach on Madden's Raider staff in 1975.

A few months earlier, Robinson had parked a motor home outside the Rose Bowl in Pasadena and kept it there for two weeks. It was used for celebrations after USC beat Michigan, 14–6, in the Rose Bowl, and after the Raiders routed Minnesota, 32–14, in Super Bowl XI on the same field eight days later.

After the Super Bowl game, Robinson went to the motor home for a magnum of champagne and presented it to Clarence Davis, a former USC running back who rushed for 137 yards against the Vikings.

"Rod Martin," Robinson said immediately when Madden called looking for a football player on draft day.

Edwards. King made a fingertip catch and went the distance, 80 yards for a touchdown, escorted by wide receiver Bob Chandler.

"The play wasn't designed for me to go deep," King said. "I'm supposed to go 6 yards upfield and cut for the sidelines, but when I saw Jim looking upfield I broke up the sideline. I didn't hear any footsteps behind me and Chandler kept up with me stride for stride. I didn't know he was that fast."

The Raiders, led by nose tackle Reggie Kinlaw and linebackers Martin, Hendricks, and rookie Matt Millen, held running back Wilbert Montgomery to 44 yards rushing.

Rod Martin had three inter-ceptions in Super Bowl XV.

Martin was an undersized linebacker, perhaps 6'2" and 220 at his biggest, who was considered too small to play in the NFL.

The Raiders listened to Robinson and selected Martin, a pick that would pay off a few years later after Madden left the sideline for the television booth.

Martin was cut by the Raiders as a rookie and wound up across the bay with the San Francisco 49ers, who also released him. He returned to the Raiders and stuck in 1978, eventually becoming a starter. He was an All-Pro selection three times in the 1980s.

In Super Bowl XV he intercepted three passes by Ron Jaworski of the Philadelphia Eagles. In Super Bowl XVIII he again played a key role as the Raiders defeated the Washington Redskins.

That phone call turned out to be a ringing success.

Plunkett completed thirteen of twenty-one passes for 261 yards and three touchdowns, two to Branch.

"Do I feel vindicated?" Plunkett, the game's most valuable player, said in response to a question afterward. "No, not really. Vindication implies bitterness and I don't feel bitterness toward anybody.

"I don't think I'm playing any better than I did in San Francisco. I still have the same confidence, I was just given the opportunity to play, and I'm with a better team."

In 1980, the best team.

Mad Bombers

The roots of the Oakland Raiders' quarterback legacy are planted in two backroads towns in California's fertile San Joaquin Valley.

Clovis, a suburb of Fresno, renamed its high school football stadium in honor of its favorite son, Daryle Lamonica, the famed "Mad Bomber," who went off to fame and fortune with Notre Dame and the Raiders.

Not to be outdone, the sleepy farming town of Sanger, several miles down the road, renamed its stadium for number one son Tom Flores, who was the first quarterback of the Raiders in 1960 and later coached the team to two Super Bowl victories.

"The Clovis High Cougars played the Sanger Apaches every year," Lamonica recalled in 2003. "We were four years apart in school, but I knew of him in high school and when he went on to play in college.

"Tom started it all with the Raiders at quarterback. He went through some real tough years in Oakland, but when I got there, everything was in place."

Flores and Lamonica are further linked in Raider lore by the 1967 trade that sent Flores and wide receiver Art Powell to the Buffalo Bills for Lamonica, who then led the Raiders to their only American Football League championship and a berth in Super Bowl II.

"It's kind of funny how things work out like that," said Flores, who went to school up the road in Stockton at University of the Pacific. "We were just two Valley kids. Clovis and Sanger were only about 15 miles apart. They keep growing, so they're getting closer.

"When I was a kid, the only reason we went to Clovis was to get into a fight on Friday nights. I was a little older than Daryle, so we never played against each other in high school, but it's interesting that two guys from the same area would be tied together like that."

Another intriguing piece of Raiders history was that in 1961, Flores's backup quarterback was Nick Papac from Fresno State. That was a reversal of their roles a few years earlier at Sanger High, where Papac was the starting quarterback and the younger Flores was his understudy.

Flores was selected by Coach Eddie Erdelatz to start at quarterback for the Raiders' first game against the Houston Oilers on September 11, 1960, and was Oakland's quarterback for most of the franchise's first seven seasons.

Tom Flores (15), throwing against the Boston Patriots at Frank Youell Field, started the Raider quarterback tradition.

Despite being sidelined for the 1962 season because of tuberculosis, Flores still ranks fourth in Raider history with ninety-two touchdown passes and set a team record that still stands when he threw six touchdown passes in a 1963 game against Houston.

"Tom Flores was such a tough guy," said Scotty Stirling, formerly public relations director and general manager of the Raiders. "Our line was not as good in the early years as it would become, but Tom would stand in the pocket forever waiting for a play to develop.

"He took a terrible beating, but he always held his ground."

That, and the fact that he once worked for an icehouse in Sanger, earned Flores his nickname, "The Iceman." His autobiography is titled, *Fire in the Iceman*.

Flores's poise in the pocket became a trademark of Raider quarterbacks, as Lamonica, George Blanda, Kenny Stabler, and Jim Plunkett all were known for their fearlessness under duress while waiting for a receiver to come open deep.

The Raiders' passing game in those days was designed for the receivers to run deeper routes and for the quarterback to take a seven-step drop, which required the offensive line to hold blocks longer. That meant the quarterback had to hold the ball longer, making him more vulnerable to the pass rush.

Rich Gannon, who has quarterbacked the Raiders into the new century, also is a picture of poise in the pocket behind an outstanding line, but is part of a different breed because of his exceptional ability to escape the rush and run with the ball.

Flores had his best season with Oakland in 1966, passing for 2,638 yards and twenty-four touchdowns, but it would turn out to be his last as a player with the Raiders.

During the off-season, he was traded for Lamonica.

"I was not happy," Flores said. "I didn't want to go to Buffalo. I had played my entire career until then with the Raiders, and I wanted to play my whole career in Oakland, but what could I do.

"What made it more difficult was I could see what was going to happen. We were good in 1966 and I knew that as the offensive line matured, the Raiders were going to make a run for the Super Bowl. I wanted to be part of it."

Instead, Lamonica stepped into the Raiders' offense, which seemed to have been created specifically for him, and led Oakland to the Super Bowl by passing for 3,227 yards and thirty touchdowns.

But at first, he too was unhappy with the trade.

"I had established myself in Buffalo and was looking forward to being the starter there," Lamonica said. "I was shocked and hurt. Then Al Davis called and said he hoped I was excited about coming to the Raiders. I went up to Oakland the next day and I got excited pretty quickly when I saw the possibilities.

"It was the best thing that could have happened to me. I got my opportunity to start with a young, emerging team, and I was on the West Coast, so my family could watch me play. It was a great time in my life."

Lamonica, who became known as "The Mad Bomber," spent the next six seasons as triggerman of the most feared passing attack in pro football, putting the bomb in Oakland's vertical passing game with his powerful right arm.

He passed for a team-record thirty-four touchdowns in 1969, tied Flores's club mark with six touchdown passes against Buffalo that season, and threw at least one touchdown pass in twenty-five consecutive games during a stretch from 1968–70.

"It was an exceptional offense because we could throw deep to not only the wide receivers, but [also to] the tight end and the running backs," Lamonica said. "Clem Daniels could come out of the backfield and outrun most defensive backs, and Al Davis turned Billy Cannon into a tight end who could do the same thing.

"When I came to the Raiders, Cotton Davidson was the best mentor. He knew the offense better than anyone, and he was my roommate. I kept him up for hours asking him questions. When he would finally go to sleep, I would stay up and study some more, and sometimes wake him up if I had any more questions."

With Lamonica, the Raiders would throw deep from anywhere on the field. If they got a turnover deep in enemy territory, or any time they moved past the 50 yard line, Lamonica would start throwing for the end zone.

Lamonica's best passing percentage for one season was 53 percent in 1972, but the Raiders didn't much care.

"Our philosophy was attack, attack, attack," Lamonica said. "If you had a weakness, we would go right after it. But it didn't matter. We had Fred Biletnikoff and Warren Wells, and later Cliff Branch, so we didn't care who they lined up against.

"We put pressure on the defenses by lining up both wide receivers on the same side of the field, in our East formation, or by flexing out our tight end, Cannon and later Raymond Chester.

"We wanted to make seven or eight big plays a game and felt we could score at least twenty-four points. That made us very tough to beat. Most teams couldn't keep up with us. It was just a great offense."

And Lamonica was the right man at the right time with his finger on the trigger.

"Daryle had that magnificent arm," Stirling said. "He had a cannon. And for a guy who could throw the ball so far, he threw to his backs so well. If you blitzed him, he would dump the ball off and our backs could really run. So you had to cover our guys straight up, which wasn't easy, and Lamonica could hit them on the numbers 50 yards away."

Though Lamonica was the unquestioned starter, the Raiders were loaded at the quarterback position with veteran George Blanda and later young Kenny Stabler in reserve.

Coach John Madden handled the situation skillfully, bringing Blanda off the bench when Lamonica was injured or in desperate situations in which Blanda more often than not worked his magic to pull out a victory.

Only when Stabler had matured to the point where he challenged Lamonica for the starting role early in the 1970s was there any hint of a quarterback controversy.

"It was a perfect situation because we had three great quarterbacks and they each gave us something different," Madden said. "Daryle Lamonica was the starter and he was one of the best quarterbacks in football. He was a great pure passer and threw a perfect, tight spiral almost every time. He threw the long pass as well as anyone who ever played.

"George Blanda was like a relief pitcher, the closer. He just knew how to play the game. It was like a chess game to him. He would watch from the sidelines and see how the game was going. When he got into the game, he knew exactly what he wanted to do. He had a quick release and he was the greatest competitor I've ever been around.

"Kenny Stabler, who was the young and developing quarterback, was as cool on the field as anyone I've ever seen. He was the same on Sunday as he was during practice on Wednesday afternoon. He didn't have a powerful arm, but he could still throw the deep pass, and he was very accurate on the short and intermediate passes.

"Lamonica started, but if we needed something else or if Lamonica was injured, we went to Blanda. But if Daryle had a long-term injury, we would have gone with Stabler. To have three guys like that at the same time was a once-in-a-lifetime situation for a coach."

Stabler broke into the starting lineup in the first game of the 1972 season at Pittsburgh, beating out Lamonica during training camp and the preseason. The young left-hander played respectably, but the offense sputtered and Lamonica came off the bench to spark the Raiders with two long touchdown passes to rookie wide receiver Mike Siani, a number one draft choice from Villanova.

The Raiders' rally came up short, 34–28, but Lamonica regained the starting job.

Madden showed that times were changing later that season when he bypassed Blanda and brought in Stabler to replace Lamonica when the Raiders were struggling in the fourth quarter of a playoff game at Pittsburgh. Stabler drove the Raiders to the go-ahead touchdown, scoring himself on a 30-yard run in the final minutes before being upstaged by Franco Harris's Immaculate Reception.

The Raiders struggled to a 1–2 start without scoring an offensive touchdown in 1973. Before a game at St. Louis, Stabler complained about his lack of playing time and asked Madden if he could run the scout team offense in practice. Stabler was so good, Madden put him into the starting lineup against the Cardinals.

"Not because he came in and bitched about not playing, but because he didn't give up and pout," Madden said. "He went out on the field and backed up his claim for the position."

Kenny Stabler led the Raiders to five consecutive AFC Championship Games.

It marked the end of one era and the start of another.

Stabler completed nineteen of thirty-one passes for 207 yards and a touchdown in a 17–10 victory over the Cardinals. Three weeks later, he broke the great Sammy Baugh's NFL record for best completion percentage in one game by hitting on twenty-five of twenty-nine passes against Baltimore— including fourteen in a row.

In his seven seasons as a starter, Stabler established nearly every Raider career passing record, though they might not hold up the way Gannon and the Raiders have been throwing the ball in recent seasons.

Stabler attributed much of it to timing.

"During most of the time when Daryle was the quarter-back, teams played mostly man-to-man defense, and his arm was a great advantage for the Raiders," Stabler said. "By the time I took over, teams were starting to play a lot of zone. I didn't have great arm strength, but my strong suit was accuracy and that gave me an advantage against zone defenses.

Kenny Stabler

Kenny "The Snake" Stabler was a throwback, out of the Bobby Layne quarterback mold, playing as hard on Saturday night as he did on Sunday afternoon.

Artie Donovan, who played defensive tackle for the Baltimore Colts, has often told the story of the day he smelled alcohol on Layne's breath in a game against Layne's Detroit Lions.

"Bobby, is that from last night?" Donovan asked.

Replied Layne: "Naw, I had a couple belts at halftime."

Stabler admits to having a few drinks to relax the night before a game, but claims he was minor league compared with Layne.

"We played together once in a celebrity golf tournament," Stabler said. "Bobby grabbed me in the lobby of the hotel and said, 'C'mon, Lefty. We have to go warm up.' He took me to the bar. It was 8 o'clock in the morning."

But Stabler, who did some of his carousing with a girl named "Wonderfully Wicked Wanda," was the standard in Oakland.

Stories would circulate in the parking lot before games at the Oakland Coliseum that Stabler had been seen partying until the wee hours the night before, anywhere from Oakland to Concord, to Pleasanton, to Alameda, even though he couldn't have been to all the bars he was supposedly spotted in.

"John Madden basically tossed me the playbook and let me do what I wanted as long as he won. And we did."

Stabler didn't really have the arm Al Davis looks for in his quarterbacks, but with him at the controls the Raiders did what Davis likes best. They won, more consistently than ever before or since.

The Raiders were 74–25 during the regular season and 7–4 in playoff games for a 73.6 winning percentage in Stabler's seasons as the starting quarterback. Oakland played in five con-

The Snake would go out and lead the Raiders to victory, then party some more.

Stabler, who came to the Raiders in 1968 as a skinny 170-pound running quarterback, started hanging out with some of the linemen and linebackers, drinking beer and lifting weights until he built up to a not-so-svelte 225 pounds.

It played well until Stabler and the Raiders struggled late in his career in Oakland. During a nightmare season in 1978, he threw only sixteen touchdown passes and thirty interceptions.

Kenny Stabler is something of a folk hero in Oakland.

Stabler heard the exaggerated stories.

"As the season went along, the fatter I got, the drunker I got, and the more women I got," said Stabler, who was traded to the Houston Oilers after the 1979 season.

Still, Stabler is a folk hero in Oakland, perhaps the most popular Raider ever.

secutive AFC Championship Games, finally breaking through and winning Super Bowl XI with Stabler running the offense.

"When Snake called a play, we knew it was the right play," tackle Art Shell said. "Because if it wasn't the right play, he wouldn't have called it."

Stabler improved his arm strength and developed good timing and touch on the long ball, especially with Cliff Branch, who had world-class speed. As for Stabler's ability to rally the Raiders to improbable victories, guard Gene Upshaw said, "We had so much confidence in him, we thought we could never lose. He had such an air of confidence, we felt we could come back no matter what the situation."

When the Raiders scored two touchdowns in the final ten minutes to beat New England in the 1976 playoffs, Upshaw said Stabler "came into the huddle with ice water in his veins. I thought to myself, 'This is why we do it all the time, because he's like that.' "

Another quarterback who inspired his teammates that way was Jim Plunkett, who was salvaged from pro football's scrap heap and led the Raiders to two Super Bowl victories.

Plunkett came to the Raiders in 1978 as a battered and beaten man, but resurrected himself to take over in 1980 after Stabler was traded to Houston and Dan Pastorini was lost for the season with a broken leg.

"We knew Jim had greatness in him," said Tom Flores, who coached the Raiders to victories in Super Bowls XV and XVIII. "He had been beaten up, benched, was out of football. But this was a guy who had made big plays in big games all his life.

"He stepped into that huddle with guys like Upshaw and Shell and took charge. He knew he belonged there and he proved it, without any chest pounding. He's the kind of guy you want to go to war with."

Even with the Raiders, Plunkett battled injuries and adversity, being benched during the 1984 season before coming back to lead his team to victory in the Super Bowl.

Plunkett ranks behind Stabler, Lamonica, and now Gannon in most Raider career passing categories, but his biggest number was an 8–3 record in postseason games, including 2–0 in AFC Championship Games and 2–0 in Super Bowls.

"The Raiders were looking for a quarterback who could throw the ball deep, a guy with a strong arm, and that was me,"

Plunkett said. "So I felt right away it was a good fit for me. I sat behind Stabler for two years, so I was healthy and fresh when I took over.

"I didn't go from being a bad quarterback to a good quarterback. I always felt I could get the job done. If I had played with the Raiders my whole career, I would have always been with a winner."

Tight end Raymond Chester, the Raiders' number one draft choice in 1980 out of Morgan State, had two stints with the Raiders: from 1970–72 before being traded to the Baltimore Colts and from 1978–81.

Chester played with all of the great Raider quarterbacks of that era.

"Blanda was the John Wayne of football," Chester said. "He was like E. F. Hutton, when he spoke in the huddle, everyone listened. George knew what he wanted to do and he didn't always stick strictly to the playbook, so in a way it was like sandlot football, but it worked.

"Everybody talks about Lamonica's arm, and he did throw the best long ball of anyone I've ever seen. But he also had the best eyes. He would spot things coming out of the huddle, before the defense even was lined up. If there was a mismatch, he would see it and exploit it.

"I could see that Snake was going to be a star when he was young. I always felt a little cheated that I didn't get to play a full season with him. I've always wondered how many passes I could have caught. I think I would be in the Hall of Fame had I played my whole career with him. He had more confidence than anybody.

"Jim Plunkett had the biggest heart, the most courage of anybody I ever played with. He had a great throwing arm, but he looked bad, even ugly out there sometimes. But he was so tough and he could make plays, big plays. He had the will to win.

"I loved all those guys and I loved playing with them."

The Raiders had high hopes for Marc Wilson after Plunkett retired following the 1986 season, but he never panned out.

Jay Schroeder led them to the 1991 AFC Championship Game, but the loss of Bo Jackson the week before was too much to overcome.

When Jeff Hostetler arrived in 1993, the Raiders finally had another quarterback with not only the ability but the toughness they were looking for.

"He's the most determined individual I've been around," Coach Art Shell said after Hostetler rallied the Raiders to a 33–30 overtime victory against the Denver Broncos in the 1993 regular season finale to earn a playoff spot.

"You can knock him down, but if you don't cut his legs off, you're going to regret it, because he's going to jump back up and be ready to go again."

Hostetler stepped in for injured Phil Simms to lead the New York Giants to victory in Super Bowl XXV, but he played in Simms's shadow for the rest of his career in New York. Finally, he had a team to call his own when he came to the Raiders.

Even though the Raiders didn't reach the playoffs again with him at quarterback, Hostetler played with toughness and distinction in his four seasons, before injuries wore him down. Hostetler passed for 11,122 yards and sixty-nine touchdowns with the Raiders, and his 424 yards passing against San Diego in 1993 was a team record until broken by Rich Gannon in 2002.

Jeff George passed for a Raider record 3,917 yards and twenty-nine touchdowns in 1997, but the Raiders finished 4–12.

The consensus was that Gannon was not the answer for the Raiders when he came to Oakland in 1999, after being a career backup at Minnesota, Washington, and Kansas City. But Coach Jon Gruden said Gannon was the perfect fit for his offense.

Gannon proved it by tying Stabler's Raider career record of 304 completions while passing for 3,840 yards and twenty-four touchdowns in his first season.

"There are certain things Rich brings to a team," Gruden said. "He is a mobile guy. He does well in crunch time. He has an aura about him. We clicked right away. I'd never been around a guy who was so passionate about playing."

The Gruden-Gannon combination was even better in 2000, when the Raiders reached the AFC Championship Game before losing to the Baltimore Ravens, 16–3.

The Raiders had it going again in 2001 before being ousted from the playoffs by a controversial 16–13 overtime loss to the New England Patriots, when a fumble recovery that would have given the victory to Oakland was overturned by replay in the final minutes of regulation.

Gruden left for the Tampa Bay Buccaneers after the season, and there were questions about whether Gannon could reach the same heights under Coach Bill Callahan.

Gannon had had three consecutive seasons of more than 3,000 yards passing and a total of seventy-nine touchdown passes, and he was confident things would not change with Jerry Rice and Tim Brown, plus a stable of young receivers.

But even he couldn't have predicted what happened.

Gannon was on an NFL-record pace with 3,195 yards after ten games and finished with an NFL-record 418 completions in 618 attempts for 4,689 yards and thirty-six touchdowns, allowing only ten interceptions. He made a run at Dan

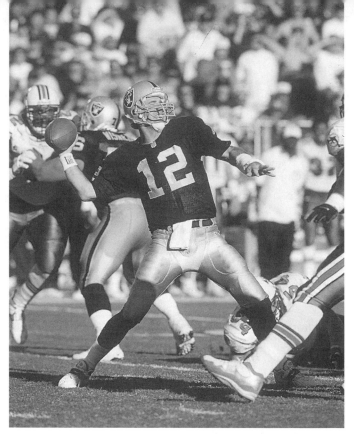

Rich Gannon (12) goes deep against the Miami Dolphins.

Marino's NFL record of 5,048 yards in a season until the Raiders reversed their offensive tendency and rushed ninety-seven times while throwing only fifty-one passes in the last two games of the regular season.

Lamonica and Plunkett shared the Raider record of ten 300-yard passing games in their careers, but Gannon did it ten times in 2002—an NFL record.

"I had no idea we were going to throw it as many times as we did," Gannon said. "I don't think our players did and I don't think our coaches did. As the season progressed, we kind of evolved into what we do best.

"I think the people around me have gotten better. There aren't many quarterbacks who can look to the right and see Tim Brown, a Hall of Fame receiver, and look to the left and see Jerry Rice, a Hall of Fame receiver.

"That's a luxury I have here."

Gannon was selected the NFL's most valuable player, joining Stabler (1974) and Marcus Allen (1985) as the only Raiders to earn that honor. More importantly, he led the Raiders to their third consecutive AFC West title, the AFC Championship, and Super Bowl XXXVII.

"I think he has a dimension that I haven't seen a quarterback take," Coach Bill Callahan said. "Here's a guy who won more games at the quarterback position in the regular season than anybody in the league [in the last three years].

"He's a player that we ask a tremendous amount from. You've seen him improve on a year-to-year basis, this year being his finest as a pro."

Rice played for Super Bowl champions in San Francisco with Joe Montana and Steve Young, two of the greatest quarterbacks in NFL history.

He sees some of the same traits in Gannon.

"He did some things this year nobody has ever done," Rice said. "Rich is the heart of our offense. He's a competitor and he's a winner. He makes plays and he does whatever it takes to win.

"In that way, he's right up there with Montana and Young. But like John Elway, until he wins a Super Bowl ring, people won't put him with those guys."

Gannon didn't get his ring to go with a brilliant 2002 season, and he isn't a California guy like Flores, Lamonica, and Plunkett, but he has proved to be a worthy successor.

Triple Crown

Super Bowl XVIII was supposed to be a coronation for the Washington Redskins, who were being hailed as perhaps the greatest team in National Football League history.

The Redskins had polished off the Miami Dolphins, 27–17, in the Super Bowl the previous year and coasted through the 1983 regular season with a 14–2 record while ringing up an astounding NFL-record 541 points.

Washington's offense had the "Hogs," a formidable offensive line, plus other assorted groups known as "the Smurfs" and "the Fun Bunch," not to mention running back John Riggins and quarterback Joe Theismann.

The Raiders listened in bemused silence during the two-week hype period between the conference championship games and the Super Bowl in Tampa, Florida.

"We had to listen to Theismann for two weeks, but that's what he does," said quarterback Jim Plunkett, who had again overcome adversity to lead the Raiders into the Super Bowl for the second time in four years.

"Our coaches told us not to say anything, to wait until game day. Two weeks is a long time, with all the media hype, and after 8–9–10 days you just want to go play the game. When the time came, we were ready."

Final score: Raiders 38, Redskins 9, the biggest and definitely the most surprising Super Bowl blowout until that time.

As dominant as the Raiders were in claiming their third Super Bowl victory, and even though they went through the

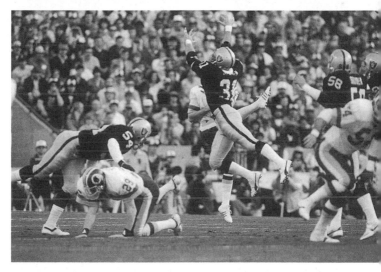

Derrick Jensen (31) blocks Jeff Hayes' punt and recovers for a TD to get the Raiders started in Super Bowl XVIII.

regular season with a 12–4 record, the 1983 season was anything but by the blueprint.

The Raiders had moved to Los Angeles in 1982, and in July 1983, Judge Nat A. Agliano in Monterey County Superior Court dismissed a suit by the city of Oakland to exercise its right of eminent domain to retain the team.

But, on the field, the Raiders were in a state of flux.

"We knew we had a good team," Coach Tom Flores said. "All the pieces were in place. But we didn't have Gene Upshaw and Art Shell for the first time in about fifteen years, and we had to replace that leadership. But we felt we had enough veterans who would step forward.

"There are ups and down in every championship season, and we didn't kill everybody we played that year, but we won some games in the fourth quarter. Great teams do that."

Plunkett, thirty-five, was one of those veterans Flores looked to for leadership, but he would have to endure another season of pain and adversity before leading the Raiders back to the pinnacle of professional football.

Even though young Marc Wilson outplayed Plunkett during training camp and the preseason, Flores went with the veteran to start the season despite a story in a Los Angeles newspaper that reported most of the Raiders wanted Wilson.

"We knew we could win with Plunkett because he had done it for us before, and we felt he still had something left," Flores said. "But we also felt we could win with Wilson if we had to turn to him.

"It was a good situation with both of them."

Things went according to plan for the first four games, victories over Cincinnati, Houston, Miami, and Denver, before the Raiders headed to Washington for what would prove to be a Super Bowl preview.

Playing without injured Marcus Allen, the Raiders rallied from a thirteen-point deficit behind Plunkett's four touchdown passes and had a 35–20 lead with seven and a half minutes remaining.

Washington was backed up on its own 12 yard line when Theismann flipped a screen pass to Joe Washington, who raced 67 yards down the right sideline. On the Raider bench defensive coordinator Charlie Sumner made a mental note of the play.

Theismann threw a touchdown pass to Charlie Brown on the next play. Then the Redskins got the ball back after Mark Moseley's onside kick bounced off the leg of Raider linebacker Jack Squirek, a name to remember. Moseley kicked a field goal and Theismann threw a 6-yard touchdown pass to Washington with thirty-three seconds remaining to give the Redskins a 37–35 victory in the NFL's regular-season game of the year.

Wasted for the Raiders were five sacks by Howie Long, a club record 97-yard punt return by Greg Pruitt, and Plunkett's 99-yard touchdown pass to Cliff Branch, who pulled a hamstring on the play and would miss more than a month.

"It's not like they blew us out," Plunkett said. "They never stopped us and we made some mistakes to let them back in it. So when we played them later, we knew we could beat them."

But first, the Raiders had to get through their toughest stretch of the season.

Two of Plunkett's first three passes against Kansas City were intercepted by cornerback Albert Lewis, but linebacker Ted Hendricks saved a 21–20 victory over the Chiefs when Long cleared a path for him to block a field-goal attempt by Nick Lowery with nine seconds left.

"I study films to find out where the weak spot is in the middle of the other team's line," said the 6'7" Hendricks, one of the most prolific kick-blockers in NFL history. "I take advantage of my height and then just get in the way of the ball."

But trouble was looming and Plunkett seemed to know it.

Fullback Frank Hawkins fumbled heading for the winning touchdown and Allen alertly recovered in the end zone.

"It was not a very productive game for us," Plunkett said. "We have to get better."

Instead, things got worse against the Raiders' nemeses, the Seattle Seahawks. The Raiders held a 17–7 lead at halftime and seemed in control when they started to unravel. Allen fumbled on the first series of the second half, quarterback Jim Zorn of the Seahawks ran 18 yards for a touchdown, and then Paul Johnson put Seattle ahead with a 75-yard punt return.

Plunkett's interception and two fumbles led to touchdowns, and when it was over Seattle, despite gaining only 153 total yards, had a 38–36 victory in the Kingdome, with the help of eight Raider turnovers.

"It was like a nightmare," Allen said. "Only this wasn't a nightmare. This was the real thing."

Two weeks later, it was the same story in the Los Angeles Coliseum.

Instead of bouncing back with a vengeance against the Seahawks, the Raiders committed five more turnovers and played probably their worst game of the season in a 34–21 defeat.

"In the two games, Seattle scored forty-five points on us without ever getting a first down," Charlie Sumner said.

In the first Seattle game, Flores had inserted Marc Wilson at quarterback in the fourth quarter, and he threw two touchdown passes before the rally fell short. Wilson was so impressive that with Plunkett and the offense struggling, Flores selected the younger of his quarterbacks to start on *Monday Night Football* against the Dallas Cowboys, who were 7–0.

"Plunkett was all beat up and we had to do something, the way we were playing," Flores said. "We were still in first place, but we needed some new life. Jim didn't like it, and I didn't expect him to like it, but he had the experience to handle it."

Wilson, rumored to be ready to jump to the New Jersey Generals of the World Football League, was signed to a five-year, $4 million deal by the Raiders in the days leading up to the Dallas game. He was right on the money at Texas Stadium, completing twenty-six of forty-nine passes for 318 yards and three touchdowns.

The Raiders were leading, 31–24, at halftime when Flores said to assistant coach Sam Boghosian as they were leaving the field, "This is a helluva game, isn't it?"

It got better in the second half.

The Raiders made it interesting again by losing five fumbles, the last by Wilson on a sack that was scooped up by linebacker Mike Hegman for a 9-yard touchdown that gave the Cowboys a 38–34 lead.

Wilson, playing his best game as a Raider, scrambled 23 yards to keep alive a drive that led to a 26-yard field goal by Chris Bahr. Then Wilson drove the Raiders again to Bahr's fourth field goal, again from 26 yards, with twenty seconds remaining to finish off a 40–38 victory.

"I'm especially pleased for Marc," Flores said. "You talk about pressure, starting your first game of the season, playing a team that's undefeated, playing on their home turf and having a game like this, taking the beating he did. I just think it was a great victory for Marc and the whole organization."

Unfortunately for Wilson, it didn't last. He threw four interceptions the following week in the second loss to Seattle. Then he suffered a broken left shoulder trying to make a tackle after an interception during a game at Kansas City.

Wilson was lost for the season and never lived up to the high hopes the Raiders had for him.

For Plunkett, it was eerily reminiscent of 1980, when Dan Pastorini suffered a broken leg, also against Kansas City, and the battered old hero stepped in and led the Raiders to a world championship.

"It was amazing what three weeks of rest did for him," Flores said. "He was like a new guy. He was fresh, crisp; he moved better in the pocket. It was like he had a shot of adrenaline or something."

Plunkett sparked a twenty-one-point explosion by the Raiders in the fourth quarter, throwing a 19-yard touchdown pass to rookie Dokie Williams for the go-ahead score in a 28–20 victory. The old warrior completed five of nine passes for 114 yards with no interceptions, no fumbles, and no sacks.

"He came in and created a spark for their offense," Coach John Mackovic of Kansas City said. "Those who have watched the Raiders and Plunkett appreciate that he can do that."

With Plunkett back in form, the Raiders won five consecutive games and clinched a spot in the playoffs, but it wasn't all that easy.

Bahr kicked a 39-yard field goal with four seconds left to overcome the Denver Broncos and rookie quarterback John Elway, 22–20. The following week there was no time left when Bahr kicked a 36-yard field goal to beat Buffalo, 27–24.

"These kind of games are going to make an old man out of me," Flores said. "They make you gray, give you an ulcer, and make you lose your hair."

In a 27–12 victory over the New York Giants, All-Pro cornerback Mike Haynes moved into the starting lineup. Haynes, acquired at midseason from the New England Patriots, gave the Raiders bookend shutdown corners with Lester Hayes on the other side. Haynes, replacing young Ted Watts, saved a touchdown against the Giants with an end zone interception.

"Ted didn't play badly at all," Flores said. "He didn't get beat for a touchdown all year. But he was playing cautious. He's not quite there yet. Mike Haynes is."

Haynes, on his way to the Hall of Fame, was the final piece to an emerging defense that in seven weeks would paralyze what was being called the most prolific offense in NFL history.

The following week, the Raiders shut down Dan Fouts and Air Coryell in a 42–10 victory over the San Diego Chargers, who took notice of what was happening.

"Their defensive backfield is absolutely great," Coach Don Coryell of San Diego said. "Great corner guys. Great athletes."

In addition to cornerbacks Hayes and Haynes, the Raiders had strong safety Mike Davis and free safety Vann McElroy in the secondary.

Davis, the hero in the 1980 playoff game in the ice at Cleveland, was still making game-saving plays. At Kansas City he stripped the ball from wide receiver Carlos Carson after a long gain, and Watts recovered on the 5 yard line to preserve a one-point lead in the fourth quarter.

McElroy, a hard-hitting second-year man from Baylor, tied for the AFC lead with eight interceptions in his first season as a starter.

After stumbling against St. Louis, 34–24, the Raiders wrapped up home-field advantage in the playoffs by trouncing the Chargers again, 30–14.

"I'm not going to be satisfied until I'm on the plane to Tampa, thinking about a ring about the size of a headlight on a car," said All-Pro defensive end Howie Long.

Across the nation, especially on the East Coast, everyone was talking about the Redskins as the playoffs approached. But sportswriter Jerry Magee of the *San Diego Union-Tribune*, in a column for *Pro Football Weekly*, wrote: "I can't remember when I felt so positively about a team entering [NFL Commissioner] Pete Rozelle's tournament as I do about the Raiders. . . . This, sir, is a football team."

Waiting in the first round of the playoffs was a familiar foe, the Pittsburgh Steelers.

"We were worried about the Steelers, more so than any other playoff team we would face," Flores said. "We had played Washington and Seattle and had a good feel for them."

Howie Long

The Raiders had one of the best defensive lines in pro football during the 1980s, and the credit has to go to defensive line coach Earl Leggett, who personally scouted the players he eventually coached and persuaded the Raiders to draft them.

All played for something less than college powerhouses and were unheralded, until they played for the Raiders.

There were Bill Pickel of Rutgers, Sean Jones of Northeastern, and Greg Townsend of Texas Christian, all of whom had long and productive careers.

And then there was Howie Long of Villanova, one of the best defensive linemen who ever played.

"Earl Leggett is responsible for Howie Long the football player, more than anyone," Long said when he was inducted into the Pro Football Hall of Fame in 2000. "If it weren't for Earl Leggett, I wouldn't be much, just another Joe Blow. And that's a fact."

Long had ninety-one and a half sacks during his thirteen-year career and could have had more had he played one position. A natural defensive end, he often played in the middle and took on two or three blockers.

The Raiders played him at every position on the defensive line, even terrorizing centers by putting him at nose tackle.

"Every day at practice it was a new position," Long recalled. "I played on the nose. I played right end, left end, left tackle, and right tackle. I couldn't understand what [Leggett] was doing at the time. A lot of people were questioning it because I wasn't settling in at one position. So how could I grow as a player?"

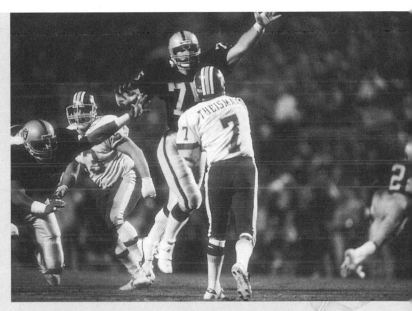

Howie Long (75) pressures Joe Theismann in Super Bowl XVIII.

Long grew enough that he was possibly the most feared lineman in football, enduring double teams and triple teams, and at times being held by offensive linemen on virtually every play.

At first Long complained long and loud to the officials about the holding, but after a while, he kept his mouth shut and played with uncommon ferocity.

When the company that cleaned and repaired the Raiders' equipment sewed up Long's torn jersey with nylon thread, he told them never to do it again, but he played the game with the shirt anyway.

Linemen trying to block Long were penalized for holding five times that day because the shirt would not rip. So Long had all of his jerseys cut and sewn at the neck and became one of the league leaders in drawing holding penalties.

But these were not the Steelers that won four Super Bowls in the 1970s.

Ailing quarterback Terry Bradshaw watched from the sideline in a baseball cap as understudy Cliff Stoudt led the Steelers to an early 3–0 lead, but after that it was no contest.

Stoudt spent the rest of the afternoon trying the escape defensive end Lyle Alzado, who had two and a half of the Raiders' five sacks.

"Alzado applied great pressure," said Coach Chuck Noll of the Steelers. "He ran over, around, and through our blockers, whatever you want to say."

Marcus Allen, beginning an incredible playoff run, ran for touchdowns of 4 and 49 yards, and Lester Hayes returned a pass interception 18 yards for another score to lead a 38–10 romp before 92,434 fans in the L.A. Coliseum on New Year's Day.

Plunkett was flawless, completing twenty-one of thirty-four passes for 232 yards. He hit wide receiver Cliff Branch six times in the first half, and when the Steelers went to double coverage outside, Plunkett found tight end Todd Christensen seven times.

"[Plunkett] has this knack for coming up with the big game when you need it most," Al Davis said.

He had another one the following week in the AFC Championship Game against Seattle, completing seventeen of twenty-four passes for 214 yards and a 3-yard touchdown pass to Allen.

But the 92,335 fans who filled the L.A. Coliseum knew the 30–14 domination of Seattle belonged to the Raider defense, which held the Seahawks to 167 yards. Alzado, who usually let his play speak for itself, set the tone when he challenged his teammates before the game.

"I thought maybe I could fire the guys up," Alzado said later.

He told his teammates: "Seattle had beaten us twice, don't forget. They've been doing a lot of talking since we played. It's important for us to take it to them right away. Manhandle them.

"It's important for us to win and not just because it's for the conference championship. They have been running off at the mouth. About how they're better than we are. Let's show them what we're made of."

Lester Hayes wasted no time, intercepting the first pass thrown by Seattle's Dave Kreig, although Hayes was called for pass interference.

Minutes later, Hayes had another interception and returned it 44 yards to the Seattle 27 yard line, setting up a field goal by Chris Bahr. It was the first of five interceptions by the Raiders, two by Mike Davis.

"I'm sure Lester shattered the guy's confidence," Mike Haynes said. "Two interceptions in one series will do that to a quarterback. I keep dreaming that I'm making a big interception and running it back. But I keep waking up and it's Lester doing it."

Fullback Frank Hawkins, whose lead-man blocking paved the way for Allen's 154 yards rushing, ran for touchdowns of 1 and 5 yards in the second quarter as the Raiders built a 20–0 halftime lead.

Alzado and Long turned AFC rushing leader Curt Warner, who was held to 26 yards rushing, to the inside, where he was consistently met by linebackers Matt Millen and Bob Nelson.

Looking ahead to the Super Bowl, Alzado said, "If we get the chance, we'll tear John Riggins' head off."

That's what happened two weeks later in Tampa, when the Raiders' humbled the heralded Washington offense.

The Raiders played a 3–4 defensive alignment, but walked up linebackers Millen and Nelson to create a five-man line. Nose tackle Reggie Kinlaw, who helped shut down Wilbert Montgomery of Philadelphia in Super Bowl XVI, was all over the field as the Raiders held Riggins to 64 yards.

"I could see the frustration in Riggins' face," Howie Long said. "I could see the fear in Theismann's face."

Theismann was sacked six times and completed only sixteen of thirty-five passes for 243 yards and two interceptions with no touchdowns, as Haynes and Hayes blanketed wide receivers Art Monk and Charlie Brown. Not only did they take Theismann's two favorite receivers out of the game, they allowed the other nine Raiders to concentrate on Riggins.

Lyle Alzado (77) and the Raiders gang up on John Riggins of the Redskins.

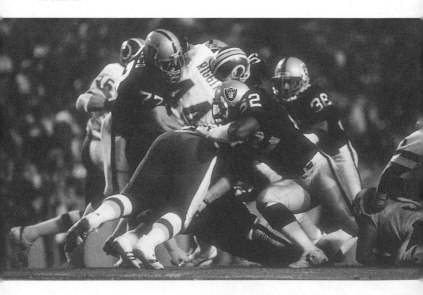

"When you have pressing corners like that, the percentage of you completing a high number of passes is not good," Theismann said. "You may beat them once in a while on a long one, but more than likely the advantage will go their way, especially as good as those two are. They don't concede the short passes. They force everything."

Not only did the big-name players come through, two unheralded Raiders helped build a 21–3 halftime lead.

Theismann was forced into three incomplete passes from the Washington 30 yard line early in the game, and Derrick Jensen, the Raiders' special teams captain, blocked Jeff Hayes's punt and recovered in the end zone for a 7–0 lead.

"I think they forgot about me," said Jensen, who was not blocked on the play.

The Raiders scored early in the second quarter when Plunkett threw 50 yards down the middle to Cliff Branch, who scored the third Super Bowl touchdown of his career by catching Plunkett's 12-yard pass two plays later.

The other two big plays in the half came courtesy of defensive coordinator Charlie Sumner, who twice remembered plays the Redskins used to beat the Raiders earlier in the season.

When Washington reached the Raiders' 7 yard line later in the second quarter, they called the same swing pass to Joe Washington that scored the winning touchdown in November. This time, Sumner called a defense that had linebacker Rod Martin there to knock the pass away, and the Redskins were forced to settle for a field goal.

But the crusher came with twelve seconds left in the half with the Redskins on their 12 yard line. Sumner called one defense, but then noticed Washington in the Redskins' huddle. Remembering the screen pass to Washington that started the Redskins' comeback earlier in the season, Sumner imme-

The Raiders mob Jack Squirek (58) after his Super Bowl touchdown.

diately grabbed reserve linebacker Jack Squirek and sent him into the game with strict instructions to follow Washington wherever he went.

The Redskins called the same screen pass, only on the other side of the field, and this time Squirek caught it and ran into the end zone for a 5-yard touchdown.

"I was surprised when they threw it," Squirek said. "I was even more surprised when I caught it."

The rest of the game was almost a formality, except for a telling sequence late in the third quarter.

Riggins gained 8 yards on first down to the Raiders' 27 yard line but couldn't get 2 more and the first down on three more runs. He was stopped on fourth-and-inches by Martin, defensive hero of Super Bowl XI with three interceptions.

"Ricky Walker [the Redskins' tight end who played at UCLA] couldn't block me in college and he can't block me now," said Martin, who attended USC.

On the next play, the last of the third quarter, Marcus Allen ran a Super Bowl–record 74 yards for a touchdown, turning what appeared to be a play going nowhere into the back-breaker.

"I was supposed to stay inside the guard on the play, but for some reason I wound up on the outside," Allen said. "Then I cut back inside, saw a huge hole, and tore upfield.

"I felt someone grab me from behind but pulled away, and then there was an alley. [Cornerback] Darrell Green didn't see me go by and I felt I could outrun the rest of the guys. It was the greatest run I've ever had on this level."

Allen finished with 191 yards rushing, which at the time was a Super Bowl record.

"Nobody ever had a better playoff run than Marcus," Flores said.

The way they dominated the Steelers, Seahawks, and Redskins, the same might be said for the Raiders.

Knowing Bo

Bo Jackson blazed across the Raider Nation like a comet. He was here one day and gone the next.

If you blinked, you missed him, like so many of the tacklers he left in his wake.

Before a freak hip injury cut short his dual professional careers, Jackson was the brightest two-sport star in the galaxy. He might have been the reincarnation of Jim Brown *and* Willie Mays.

"Jim Brown is the player you compare all backs to and Bo certainly was comparable," said Art Shell, who was Jackson's coach in 1989 and 1990, the last two of Jackson's four partial seasons with the Raiders.

"Bo had that same incredible combination of speed and power, but I think he was faster. The first time I saw him was in his first practice with the Raiders [in 1987]. He got the ball on a sweep and it looked like he was going to get clobbered. But he outran the angle and turned the corner.

"Everybody looked at each other like, 'Did you see that.' It was the first time he touched the ball and you could see he was something special."

Jackson's average of 5.4 yards per carry was better than Brown's National Football League career record of 5.2, but Bo fell 235 carries short of the 750 needed to qualify for the mark. Mercury Morris, who averaged 5.1, and Gale Sayers, at 5.0, were the only other players to average 5 yards per carry for their careers.

And you can make a theoretical case that Jackson was in the ballpark with some of baseball's greatest players.

Hank Aaron hit a record 755 home runs in 12,364 at-bats, and Mays, considered by many to be the greatest all-around player of all-time, belted 660 in 10,881.

If Jackson's 141 homers in 2,393 at-bats are multiplied by five, they project to 705 home runs in 11,965 at-bats.

ESPN's Peter Gammons said while Jackson was playing: "Everyone's babbling about Bo. They're comparing him with Willie Mays, Babe Ruth, Ted Williams, Henry Aaron, and Mickey Mantle. . . . At times it seems that this 6'1", 222-pound superhero came to baseball straight out of a Marvel Comic."

Jackson had similar speed, power and the strong throwing arm that Mays possessed, but at nearly 6'2" and 230 pounds he was much bigger than the 5'11", 180-pound Mays—probably the most instinctive baseball player in history.

"Had Bo dedicated himself to baseball, he would have been one of the best of all time," said George Brett, the Hall of Fame third baseman, who was Jackson's teammate with the Kansas City Royals. "He was the best athlete I've ever seen. Bo is my hero."

When Jackson came out of Auburn as the 1986 Heisman Trophy winner, there was speculation that he might challenge some of Brown's records—if he could have a long and reasonably injury-free career.

Jackson also was an outstanding outfielder for three years at Auburn, after being drafted out of high school by the New York Yankees. But most people dismissed his talk of playing both sports professionally as a ploy for contract leverage with the Tampa Bay Buccaneers—who made him the first pick in the NFL draft.

Bo Jackson runs over a Denver Broncos defensive back.

"My first love is baseball and it has always been a dream of mine to be a major league player," Jackson said.

Bo showed he was serious by signing with the Royals, who selected him in round four of baseball's free-agent draft, after acrimonious negotiations with owner Hugh Culverhouse of the Buccaneers.

"I might not have even pursued baseball had I been drafted by a reputable football organization," Jackson said. "[The Buccaneers] won only two games in the previous two years and those were flukes. I was very unimpressed by the organization.

"Plus, when I went to Tampa for a visit, they flew me down on Culverhouse's jet. They assured me they had checked with the NCAA and everything was OK. When I got back to Auburn the next day and dressed for baseball practice, the coach told me the NCAA had declared me ineligible for my senior year of baseball because it was a rules violation.

"That really soured me. I told them not to draft me, but they did anyway."

When Jackson showed up at Royals Stadium in Kansas City and was introduced to the media, he handed out autographed pictures of himself in his football uniform to his teammates-to-be in the Royals' locker room.

Most of the veterans were not impressed . . . yet.

"A lot of the guys laughed and threw the pictures in the garbage," Brett recalled. "But I could see the possibilities. I put mine up in my locker."

Jackson played only fifty-three games in the minor leagues with the Memphis Chicks before being recalled by the Royals and on September 14, 1986, he hit his first major league home run—a 475-foot shot that is still the longest ever hit at Royals Stadium.

In 1987, his first full season in the majors, Jackson batted .235 with 22 home runs and 53 runs batted in.

That spring, owner Al Davis of the Raiders pulled one of his seemingly annual draft surprises by selecting Jackson in the seventh round.

"Considering what he did in a short period of time and what he could have done, that was probably one of the greatest picks in the history of the draft," Raider executive Al LoCasale said. "And Bo might not have played at that point for anybody but Al and the Raiders."

"It was a perfect fit for me," Jackson said. "I bought into the whole Silver-and-Black thing, the baddest kids on the block, that suited my personality. They had a history, great players and Super Bowl championships.

"It was the Al Davis mentality. The first time we met, he called me Vincent [Jackson's given name] and I didn't answer him at first. Then I told him I sleep with the only person who calls me that, meaning my wife. He laughed and called me Bo.

"I have the utmost respect for Mr. Davis. He is the only owner I've seen with the balls to stand up for his players."

Jackson signed with the Raiders and said he would join the team, which had moved from Oakland to Los Angeles in 1982, in October, when the baseball season was over. He also said football would be his "hobby."

Some people questioned if Jackson could be successful in both sports, but he said, "I don't know why not. I have been doing it most of my life."

Until then, he had been the most popular player in Kansas City.

"The fans in Kansas City didn't like me so much after that," said Jackson, who would be coming to town once a year with the Raiders, hated rivals of the Kansas City Chiefs.

Jackson joined the Raiders, who already had one of the greatest backs in NFL history, Marcus Allen. But the Raiders immediately saw what they had and found ways to get Jackson on the field. In his fifth game of professional football, he showed the rest of the nation.

The Raiders were playing the Seattle Seahawks on *Monday Night Football* and linebacker Brian Bosworth, the former All-American at Oklahoma, was talking all week about what he was going to do to Jackson.

"Boz [was] saying he was going to do this to Bo and that to Bo," said fullback Tommy Agee of the Seahawks, who blocked for Jackson at Auburn. "I didn't say anything, but I had an idea of what was going to happen."

Bosworth didn't know it, but he was playing right into

Jackson's hands by challenging him. Jackson felt he had been proving people wrong all his life and took any perceived slight personally.

When he was being recruited by both Alabama and Auburn while at McAdory High in McCalla, Alabama, an Alabama assistant told Bo if he went to Auburn, he would never play on a team that defeated the Crimson Tide.

As a freshman at Auburn, he scored the winning touchdown as the Tigers beat Alabama for the first time in ten years.

"You didn't tell him what he couldn't do," Shell said. "When players would talk during the week about what they were going to do to him, they would always pay. He would start talking in the third person, 'They think they can stop Bo, but Bo will show them.'

"And he always did."

Not only did Jackson show Bosworth, he celebrated his birthday by putting on a show for a national television audience, rushing for a Raider record 221 yards to shatter the mark of 200 set by Clem Daniels in 1963.

The score was tied, 7–7, in the second quarter when Jackson took a pass from Marc Wilson and ran All-Pro safety Kenny Easley off his feet on a 14-yard touchdown. Minutes later, he took the air out of the Kingdome by sweeping left and running 91 yards for a touchdown.

"It was like being at Longacres [race track] and watching the horses race to the wire," said Steve Largent, the great Seattle wide receiver. "When he ran by, I felt the same surge. It was just amazing. I think he should stick to baseball."

Jackson was running so fast at the end of his run that he ran through the end zone and went up the tunnel leading off the field, and momentarily was out of sight.

Marcus Allen

Even though Marcus Allen of USC won the 1981 Heisman Trophy after becoming the first back in college football history to rush for more than 2,000 yards in a season, gaining 2,342, some people thought he was not fast enough to be successful in the National Football League.

Not the Raiders.

"I coached Marcus in the Gold Bowl in San Diego, an all-star game that was played only that one time," said Tom Flores, who coached the Raiders to victories in Super Bowls XV and XVIII. "We didn't time him in the 40-yard dash, but we could see he was fast enough.

"We watched film on him at USC and noticed that he never got caught from behind. And he could do so many things at the highest level—run, block, catch the ball, and throw the ball. It was easy to see he was a great player."

Allen would make the Pro Bowl in five of his first six years with the Raiders, was the NFL's most valuable player in 1984, and was most valuable player of Super Bowl XVIII, when he rushed for 191 yards—which at the time was a record in football's ultimate game.

The Raiders knew Allen was the man they wanted in the first round on draft day in 1982, but had to sweat out the first nine picks before their turn came at number ten.

They breathed easier as the Minnesota Vikings, also in the market for a running back, chose Darrin Nelson of Stanford with the fifth pick and exhaled when the Atlanta Falcons selected running back Gerald Riggs of Arizona State at number nine.

Owner Al Davis stepped out of a courtroom in San Francisco, where the NFL was fighting his move of the Raiders to Los Angeles, and into a phone booth. He spoke with Ron Wolf, the Raiders' draft genius, who would later build the Green Bay Packers into a Super Bowl champion.

"We're on the clock," Wolf said.

Davis: "Is he still there?"

Wolf: "Yes."

Davis: "What are you waiting for?"

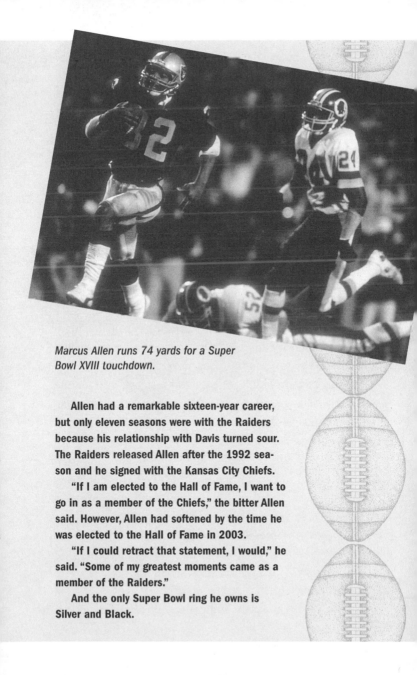

Marcus Allen runs 74 yards for a Super
Bowl XVIII touchdown.

Allen had a remarkable sixteen-year career,
but only eleven seasons were with the Raiders
because his relationship with Davis turned sour.
The Raiders released Allen after the 1992 season and he signed with the Kansas City Chiefs.

"If I am elected to the Hall of Fame, I want to
go in as a member of the Chiefs," the bitter Allen
said. However, Allen had softened by the time he
was elected to the Hall of Fame in 2003.

"If I could retract that statement, I would," he
said. "Some of my greatest moments came as a
member of the Raiders."

And the only Super Bowl ring he owns is
Silver and Black.

Unfortunately for Bosworth and the Seahawks, he came back.

"I saw the defender had the angle on me and I just threw my head back and ran for my life," Jackson said. "Try to stop after running 90-some yards in a 10-yard space. You can't do it carrying 230 pounds."

Jackson put an exclamation mark on his night by running 42 yards to set up a 2-yard touchdown run on which he ran over Bosworth at the goal line.

The Raiders, who were going nowhere in that strike-shortened season, routed the Seahawks, 37–14, to win at the Kingdome for the first time since 1981. But about all anyone remembers are the touchdown runs by Jackson.

"He just flat-out ran my butt over," said Bosworth, who likened Jackson to a freight train. "My hat's off to him."

Jackson remembers a Raiders' assistant coach making a big deal in a team meeting the next day about another game he saw Jackson play.

It seems Jackson didn't get back to his home in Redondo Beach until 3:00 A.M. after the flight from Seattle. He immediately went to sleep but had to wake up a few hours later to take care of his two-year-old son.

Jackson and his son walked 2 blocks to the Redondo Beach Pier at about 7:00 A.M. to buy a newspaper. The assistant coach drove by and saw Jackson, only hours after lighting up *Monday Night Football*, playing peek-a-boo behind a palm tree.

"That's what I remember, because I always had my priorities in order," Jackson said. "My family was always the most important thing to me, and still is. Baseball and football were only important when I was on the field."

Jackson recalls another game that like his career is a might-have-been.

In 1991 against the New Orleans Saints at the Superdome, Jackson swept right on his first carry and gained about 40 yards. On his next carry he swept left and ripped off some 40 more. On a third carry he ran for 10 yards, but came up limping.

"I slightly pulled a hamstring," Jackson said. "I had 92 yards on three carries and that was it. That really upset me. In some ways it was more disappointing than when I was injured and couldn't play football anymore. But that's life. You have to get over those bumps and move on."

Said LoCasale: "Bo might have run for 300 or 400 yards that night."

The high-water mark of Jackson's double careers was 1989, when he established himself in both sports as more than a player with unlimited potential by putting up superstar numbers.

Jackson had become the Royals' regular left fielder in 1988 by batting .246 with 25 home runs and 68 runs batted in, not to mention 27 stolen bases, but in 1989 he raised the bar. He batted .256 with 32 home runs, 105 RBIs and 26 stolen bases. Not only did he make the American League All-Star team, he was voted most valuable player of the All-Star Game at Anaheim.

Batting leadoff for the A. L., Jackson hit the second pitch from Rick Reuschel of the Chicago Cubs off his shoe tops and onto the green hitter's background behind the center field fence—a drive of close to 500 feet.

"When the ball hit the bat, it sounded like he hit a golf ball," said National League manager Tommy Lasorda of the Los Angeles Dodgers.

Jackson also hit a run-scoring single, stole a base, and robbed Pedro Guerrero of a two-run double by making a spectacular catch in left-center field as the A.L. won, 5–3.

When the baseball season ended, Jackson reported to the Raiders five games after the season started and rushed for 950 yards and four touchdowns in eleven games.

Jackson was firmly established as a two-sport star and an American folk hero, so Nike took advantage of this with its "Bo Knows" promotion.

"We were sitting in a meeting with the Nike people and someone made a point, so I said, 'I know,' " Jackson recalled. "And so the guy says, 'Oh, Bo knows.' So I say, 'Yes, Bo does know.' And that's how it all started."

Jackson, the ultimate cross-trainer, was featured in a series of commercials playing baseball, football, basketball, and even hockey. He also was shown as a jockey and a bicyclist looking for the Tour de France.

"Bo knows baseball," Kirk Gibson says in one spot.

"Bo knows basketball, too," Michael Jordan says in another.

After a clip shows Jackson in hockey gear mixing it up on the boards, a disbelieving Wayne Gretzky comes on shaking his head and says, "No."

"That was good, a fun ride," Jackson said.

Little did anybody know, the ride was almost over.

In 1990 injuries limited Jackson to 111 games with the Royals, but he batted .272 with 28 home runs and 78 RBIs.

He reported late again for football and rushed for 698 yards and five touchdowns in ten games, helping the Raiders win six of their last seven games to claim the AFC West title and make the playoffs.

Jackson rushed for 77 yards in six carries in a 20–10 play-off victory over the Cincinnati Bengals, but his football career came to a screeching halt when he was tackled from behind by linebacker Kevin Walker after a long run.

"My leg stopped and my hip kept going," Jackson said. "I

knew my hip was dislocated and I snapped it back into place while I was lying on the ground. I thought it might be like a hip pointer, but when I stood up and tried to walk, it was like somebody was jamming an ice pick into my pelvic cup.

"I knew then it might be more serious than I first thought."

Jackson tried to walk off the field by himself, but after a few steps, he retreated to the ground and waited for help.

After the game, Jackson claimed the injury was not serious and that he would play the next week in the AFC Championship Game at Buffalo, but there was no way. The Bills trounced the disheartened Raiders, 51–3.

"I don't know if Bo would have made a difference in that game," Shell said. "But it was cold that day in Buffalo, and I

Bo Jackson's football career ended on this tackle by Kevin Walker of Cincinnati.

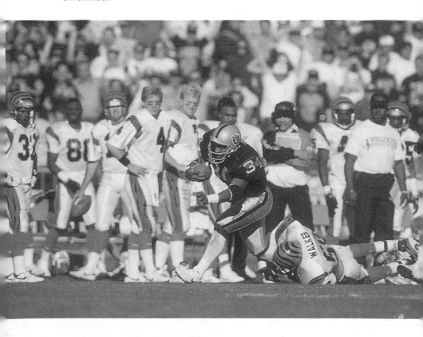

know that there would not have been any of the Bills' players anxious to tackle Bo. I'll always believe he would have run through a lot of tackles and had a big game."

Jackson never played football again because of the condition in his left hip, known as avascular necrosis, which led to deterioration of the cartilage and bone around the joint.

The Royals, never enamored with his off-season hobby, cut Jackson during spring training, and although he played parts of three more seasons with the Chicago White Sox and California Angels, he never fully regained his speed or his skills.

"I've never been squeamish, but when I saw the X ray [the day after the injury], and the doctor told me the dark stuff in the hip socket was blood, I got light-headed," Jackson said. "I had to sit down.

"It took me quite a while to get over not being able to play football again."

Jackson had hip-replacement surgery after the 1991 baseball season and couldn't play in 1992, but he vowed to return.

Before his beloved mother, Florence Jackson Bond, died in 1992, Bo made two promises to her: that he would play baseball again and that he would return to Auburn and get his degree.

He did both.

Jackson returned to the White Sox in 1993, and with his typical flair he hit a home run off Neal Heaton of the New York Yankees in his first at bat.

"That was for my mother," Jackson said. "I told her that when I went back, my first hit would be for her."

On December 11, 1995, he received his degree from Auburn.

"I cried," he said.

Jackson retired after batting .279, the highest average of

his career, and hitting 13 home runs in 201 at bats in 1994.

He left baseball a scrapbook of snapshots that included his All-Star Game home run, running up and down the left-field fence while catching a fly ball in Baltimore, hitting a home run to clinch the American League West title for the White Sox in 1993, and throwing out speedy Harold Reynolds of the Seattle Mariners with a Herculean throw from the warning track to home plate.

Jackson has three of the four longest runs in Raider history—92, 91, and 88 yards—and is the only player in NFL history to have two runs over 90 yards.

"I think it was something of a tragedy for football," Shell said. "Football missed the things he might have done. The moment Bo got hurt and couldn't play again, football lost something.

"John Madden always used to talk about the Raiders being able to score from anywhere on the field. He meant in the passing game. When we had Bo, we could strike from anywhere in the passing game and the running game. There are not too many backs who give you that."

Without Jackson, Shell's Raiders lost close games in the playoffs to Kansas City in 1991 and to Buffalo in 1993, then just missed the playoffs by losing to the Chiefs in the last game of the 1994 season.

Then Shell lost his job.

"If Bo Jackson didn't get hurt, I think Art might still be the coach of the Raiders," said Gene Upshaw, the former All-Pro guard who is executive director of the NFL Players Association. "It was a shame the way Bo's career ended. He could have been one of the best backs who ever played."

But all that Jim Brown and Willie Mays stuff never meant much to Jackson.

Jackson has been inducted into the College Football Hall of Fame in South Bend, Indiana, but he will never make it to Canton or Cooperstown.

He doesn't care.

"When people tell me I could be the best athlete there is, I just let it go in one ear and out the other," Jackson said. "There is always somebody out there who is better than you are. I never set out to be a Hall of Fame baseball player or Hall of Fame football player. I just loved to play. Period."

All he wanted was to be Bo Jackson, and that was better than most.

Return to Glory

W hen popular and dynamic young coach Jon Gruden left for the Tampa Bay Buccaneers before the 2002 season, there were dire predictions that the Oakland Raiders' resurgence went with him.

After all, the Raiders hadn't been to the Super Bowl since the 1983 season, and in his four seasons, Gruden had taken the Raiders to their first AFC Championship Game since 1991, and only one of the most controversial calls in pro football history had kept them out of another.

Everyone could see the single-minded similarities between Gruden and the man who gave him his first opportunity to coach a pro football team, owner Al Davis of the Raiders. But when Gruden, thirty-eight, expressed an interest in moving home to Tampa, where his parents live, Davis let him go.

"I asked Jon if he really wanted to go to Tampa and he said he did," Davis said. "We let Jon make the decision. If he wanted to go, we'd let him, provided we got our demands."

Make no mistake, Davis would do it all over again, despite the fact that Gruden in his first season in Tampa led the Buccaneers to Super Bowl XXXVII, where they defeated the Raiders, 48–21, at Qualcomm Stadium in San Diego.

In exchange for Gruden, the Raiders received first- and second-round draft choices in 2002. With their two first-round picks in 2002, the Raiders selected cornerback Phillip Buchanon and linebacker Napoleon Harris, who helped the Raiders reach the Super Bowl as rookies.

Oakland also got a number one pick in 2003, a number two selection in 2004, and $8 million in cash over three seasons.

Davis, whose own coaching turned the Raiders' ship in the right direction in 1963, hasn't always hired the right man for the job since then, but more often than not he has.

When Davis went to New York to be commissioner of the American Football League, John Rauch was promoted to head coach of the Raiders. When Davis lost Rauch to the Buffalo Bills, he promoted John Madden. When Madden retired, Davis promoted Tom Flores. When Mike Shanahan struggled, Davis promoted Art Shell.

All came, if you hadn't noticed, from within the Raider organization.

When Gruden went to Tampa, most of his staff remained in Oakland and Davis named Bill Callahan, offensive coordinator and line coach, "captain" of the coaching staff. Several players lobbied for Davis to make the appointment of Callahan, who came with Gruden from the Philadelphia Eagles and remains a close friend of his former boss, a permanent one.

After a three-week observation period, Davis complied.

"I wanted to see Bill function in that role to see how the organization would operate, see how we would do in the free-agent market," Davis said. "While he hasn't been out front, as one player said, he's been a great part of the motor that drives this organization on the football field."

Callahan had been an assistant coach in the National Football League for seven seasons, but this was his first head coaching job on any level. All he did in his first season was take the Raiders to the Super Bowl, something no coach had done for nineteen seasons.

Although his coaching philosophy is similar to the charismatic Gruden's, his personality is not. That might have been important to the Raider Nation, but it rubbed some people the wrong way, including some of the players.

"I'm not concerned about the effect of charisma or what people think about that," Callahan said at his news conference after accepting the position. "I'm more concerned about our team being charismatic on the field. I'm more concerned that the product on the field is an exciting product."

That's another area where Callahan and Gruden take varying paths, even though they work out of basically the same playbook. Perhaps surprisingly, Gruden is a bit conservative, while Callahan employs a more wide-open offense.

In his first season as coach, Callahan had quarterback Rich Gannon on pace to break Dan Marino's NFL record for passing yards in a season.

Observers also came to expect the unexpected from Callahan. With Gannon in sight of the record, the Raiders went predominantly to the run in their last two games of the season, although a driving rainstorm dictated that in one game. Another example of doing the unexpected came in week two on a Sunday night at Pittsburgh, against a team that led the NFL in total defense in 2001 but had its secondary exposed in the opener when Tom Brady of New England threw forty-three passes, putting the ball in the air on twenty-five consecutive plays at one point.

The Raiders had rushed for more than 200 yards and passed for more than 200 in an opening 31–17 victory over Seattle, and Callahan said he was pleased with the balance.

Callahan said before the game in Pittsburgh that the Raiders certainly wouldn't try to mimic New England's offense, and they didn't. They outdid it. Gannon, throwing mostly out of a no-huddle offense that prevented the Steelers from making situational substitutions, completed forty-three passes, throwing sixty-four times for 403 yards in a 30–17 victory.

"The plan going in was to throw, it always was and it always has been," Callahan said. "The players knew that. We had to be aggressive and we had to attack."

The Raiders threw on seventeen of their first eighteen plays and on number nineteen Gannon gave the ball to Charlie Garner on a draw play. He ran 36 yards for a touchdown against the stunned Steelers, who were looking for another pass.

"With their [defensive] scheme, they bring so many guys from so many different places it's hard to run the ball," wide receiver Jerry Rice of the Raiders said. "We knew we had to utilize the no-huddle and we had success with it."

Terry Kirby returned a kickoff 96 yards for a touchdown when the Steelers got close in the second half, and free-agent safety Rod Woodson recovered three fumbles against his former team as Oakland won for the second time in a 4–0 start.

After a bye, the Raiders had many happy returns the next week in Oakland, with Kirby and Buchanon returning punts for touchdowns and Rod Woodson taking one of his three interceptions 82 yards for a score in a 52–25 victory over the Tennessee Titans.

Woodson surpassed Dick "Night Train" Lane to become the NFL's all-time leader for interception return yardage, and Jerry Rice passed Walter Payton for the most yardage from scrimmage in league history.

"When you're in the right place at the right time, good things happen to you," Woodson said.

Gannon completed twenty-nine of thirty-nine passes to nine receivers for 381 yards, and the Raiders had six players

Rookie Coach Bill Callahan, with quarterback Rich Gannon, took the Raiders to Super Bowl XXXVII.

carry the ball, although the running game continued to be an afterthought.

The Raiders were giving opponents plenty to think about.

"It's a lot of fun, obviously," Gannon said. "One thing we're doing a good job of is rolling a lot of personnel onto the field."

It was more of the same the following week in Buffalo, where Gannon completed twenty-three of thirty-eight passes for 357 yards and three touchdowns, in addition to running 1 yard for another score to outgun Drew Bledsoe, who passed for 417 yards, as the Raiders won, 49–31.

Buchanon, starting his second game with cornerback Charles Woodson injured, proved to be a ballhawk, making his second interception and returning it 81 yards for a touchdown. He dropped another potential interception from Bledsoe, after having one overturned by an official the previous week.

Emerging wide receiver Jerry Porter, benefiting from playing alongside Rice and Tim Brown, caught seven passes for 117 yards and a 29-yard touchdown to open the scoring.

"We still haven't showed you everything," Porter promised. "There's a lot of things that we haven't had a chance to get to because of situations. . . . You haven't seen half of it yet."

But there was trouble on the horizon.

Garner rushed eight times for 96 yards, including a 36-yard touchdown, and caught four passes for 83 yards, including a 69-yard touchdown, but pulled a hamstring on the play. He wouldn't miss any games, but it would be a while before he and the offense would be the same.

The following week in St. Louis, Gannon hit Rice for a 53-yard gain on the Raiders' first play from scrimmage, but short-yardage back Zack Crockett was stopped on fourth down on the 3 yard line. The Raiders never got untracked after that, and third-string quarterback Marc Bulger led the previously winless Rams to a 28–13 victory to start Oakland on a four-game losing streak.

Playing for the AFC West lead the following week in Oakland, the Raiders sputtered in the red zone for the second consecutive game and fell in overtime to the San Diego Chargers, 27–21. Not only that, Buchanon suffered a broken left wrist and was lost for the rest of his rookie season, and Kirby likewise was lost for the year with a broken leg. That left the Raiders without their two best cover corners and their two top kick returners.

Just when it seemed things couldn't get worse, they did.

Gannon passed for 334 yards but the problems in the red zone persisted in a 20–10 loss at Kansas City. Then the Raiders seemingly tried to satisfy their critics and failed in an effort to establish the running game, leading to a 23–20 loss in overtime to the San Francisco 49ers.

"We can't listen to what anybody else says," Porter said after the 49er game. "If we feel we have to pass on every play to win, then that's what we have to do."

The outside perception of Callahan had swung dramatically from a coach who couldn't fill the shoes he had inherited, to a budding genius, to a guy without a clue in a matter of eight weeks.

Inside the organization the perception was something entirely different.

"During that stretch in October [when the Raiders went from 4–0 to 4–4], everyone was looking at Bill," Gannon said after the Raiders won the AFC West. "I was looking at Bill. I was looking to see how he'd respond, how he'd react. He didn't waver. He talked about it each and every week. And the players believed in him and believed in what he had talked about, and that's really the reason we're all here today."

More doom was predicted when the Raiders headed for a Monday night game at Denver, with a rematch of the previous season's controversial playoff game against the Super Bowl champion New England Patriots to follow in Oakland.

Games often turn on one play, but not an entire season.

The Broncos, who had great success against the Raiders under Coach Mike Shanahan, were driving late in the first quarter, when old pro Rod Woodson stepped in front of Brian Griese's pass intended for Clinton Portis. Woodson caught the ball and ran 98 yards for a touchdown, extending his NFL record to twelve scores on interceptions and increasing the lead to 10–0.

Gannon did the rest, completing twenty-one consecutive passes at one point, twenty-nine of his first thirty, and thirty-four of thirty-eight in the game for 352 yards and three touchdowns in a 34–10 victory, only the Raiders' third in fifteen games against Shanahan.

Rice had nine receptions for 103 yards and two touchdowns, passing Walter Payton to set an NFL record for total yards and becoming the first player with 200 touchdown catches.

The Raiders won their next five games and seven of the last eight to win the AFC West and wrap up home-field advantage in the playoffs. It may not be quite that simple, but just as the problems of their four-game losing streak can be traced to a failed fourth down in St. Louis, the turnaround began with Woodson's interception.

"I'm not a fortune-teller," Woodson said as the playoffs approached. "I can't go into the past and say what would happen. Was that part of our turnaround? Yeah. Was it the only thing that happened to us? No.

"I'm glad it wasn't 101 yards. I was running out of gas. I

Rod Woodson turned the Raiders' season around by returning an interception 98 yards for a touchdown against Denver.

needed oxygen. Honest, I don't think [Griese] ever saw me. He looked me off for a second, but I don't think he ever saw me sneaking back in."

Gannon put things in perspective in the euphoria of the locker room in Denver when he said: "It was a big win but we can't start looking at the standings. We certainly can't get carried away with another big game coming up this weekend."

That's the way the Raiders approached each game the rest of the way.

Oakland took advantage of a fumble the next week by Tom Brady, whose fumble in the 2001 playoffs was overturned by the infamous "tuck rule," and the Raiders turned back the New England Patriots, 27–20.

The Oakland defense, which started the season with only cornerback Charles Woodson in the position he played the previous year, was rounding into shape and allowed only two field goals and 195 total yards.

The additions of safety Rod Woodson, tackles John Parrella and Sam Adams, and linebacker Bill Romanowski through free agency were paying off, in addition to the play of several young players. Although critical observers were quick to point out how the defense aged almost overnight with those veteran additions, it actually got younger in several positions, especially at linebacker.

William Thomas retired and Greg Biekert was waived, making room at linebacker for young playmakers Eric Barton and Napoleon Harris. Rod Woodson had to be the defensive MVP, but Barton might have been the most consistent player on the unit.

Defensive linemen DeLawrence Grant and safety Derrick Gibson also made the defense younger.

"We think we have a good mix," Davis said. "We have

some older players, but at every position we think we have some great young players, too."

Gannon continued his assault with 340 passing yards, and the Oakland ground game continued to improve when Garner gained 100 yards and Tyrone Wheatley added 87 in a 41–20 victory at Arizona.

All-Pros Barret Robbins and Lincoln Kennedy anchored a line, which also included Frank Middleton, Mo Collins, and Barry Sims, that was doing the heavy work for the run and pass.

In a playoff preview, the Raiders rebounded from a sluggish start after Tim Brown made reception number 1,000 of his career and Oakland went on to a 26–20 victory on *Monday Night Football*. Brown joined teammate Jerry Rice and Cris Carter as the only players with 1,000 catches, and Gannon threw a 36-yard touchdown pass to Rice on the next play that put the Raiders ahead to stay, 13–10.

"That's Jerry Rice," Brown said. "Every time he catches a ball, he's stealing your thunder. It's just great to have him here."

Gannon passed for 351 yards, tying an NFL record with his ninth game of the season over 300, and Sebastian Janikowski, leading the NFL in touchbacks on kickoffs, added four field goals.

The thirty-seven-year-old Gannon did not have a touchdown pass or an interception the next week, but he broke the record by passing for 328 yards in a 27–7 victory over fading San Diego, giving the Raiders sole possession of the AFC West lead. On the way to victory, the Raiders intercepted three of Drew Brees' passes and held LaDainian Tomlinson to 57 yards rushing.

"This was definitely one of our best games because no matter what they did out there, no matter what running play, no matter what passing play, we always felt like we were in control," Romanowski said.

After a 23–17 loss at Miami in which Gannon passed for only 204 yards, the Raiders claimed their third consecutive division title with a 28–16 victory over the Denver Broncos. Gannon passed for a pedestrian 201 yards but broke Warren Moon's NFL record with his 405th completion of the season.

The Raiders ran for 280 yards, 135 by Charlie Garner, in the rain to trounce Kansas City, 24–0, in the finale.

"How's that for balance?" Callahan asked after the game, giving critics a little needle. "We passed sixty times in one game and ran sixty times in another one."

With a bye in the first round of the playoffs, cornerbacks Charles Woodson and Tory James had time to recover from surgery for similar hairline ankle fractures. Both were sharp in a 20–10 victory over the Jets and young quarterback Chad Pennington to open the playoffs.

Woodson and his teammates were upset that Pennington was getting so much attention leading up to the game, even more than Gannon, who had been selected the NFL's most valuable player.

The New York media was comparing Pennington with Joe Namath and Joe Montana.

"We were calling him 'Broadway Chad,'" Charles Woodson said. "But we had the MVP in our locker room."

Pennington, a picture of poise since taking over from Vinny Testaverde early in the season, looked rattled while completing only twenty-one of forty-seven passes for 183 yards with two interceptions. He was sacked four times, twice by defensive tackle Rod Coleman, who led the Raiders with eleven sacks during the regular season even though he was not a starter.

Gannon completed twenty of thirty for 283 yards and touchdowns of 29 yards to Porter and 9 yards to Rice.

"These opportunities are few and far between," Gannon

said. "I am trying to seize the moment, seize the opportunity. Of course three other teams are trying to do the same thing."

The Tennessee Titans returned to Oakland for the AFC Championship Game, nothing new for the Raiders, who would be playing in their fourteenth title game, more than any other AFC team.

Of course they've lost more too, a total of ten.

"We've been this far before," said Porter, who caught six passes for 123 yards. "It's time to go farther. We suffered a big letdown my rookie year [2000] in the AFC championship when Baltimore came in here."

Despite a heroic performance by ailing quarterback Steve McNair of the Titans, it didn't happen again.

McNair ran for two touchdowns, one to give the Titans a 17–14 lead with 6:07 left in the first half, but Gannon again played like the MVP in leading the Raiders to a 41–24 victory.

Gannon threw a 1-yard touchdown pass to emerging rookie tight end Doug Jolley with twenty-eight seconds left in the half to put Oakland ahead to stay. Later, he ran 3 yards for a score.

"This team was built to win now and we've done that, so we're going to the Super Bowl," said Romanowski, who has four Super Bowl rings from his days in San Francisco and Denver.

Ah, yes, the Super Bowl, where there was anything but a perfect ending for the Raiders.

The first indication that it would not be their day came when All-Pro center Barret Robbins disappeared Friday night from the team's hotel in La Jolla and did not reappear until late the following day.

Robbins, who has bipolar disorder, apparently stopped taking his medicine and was incoherent when he returned. The Raiders turned him over to his agent and family, who had Robbins hospitalized.

Jerry Rice and Tim Brown

When Jerry Rice ran a crossing pattern over San Francisco Bay in 2001, there was speculation that the greatest receiver in NFL history and new teammate Tim Brown might soon be taking shots at each other.

And they were.

Rice and Brown became fast friends, on and off the field with the Oakland Raiders, but that friendship apparently does not extend to the golf course, where team members play a weekly game on their day off throughout football season.

"When Jerry came here [after not being re-signed by the San Francisco 49ers], there was some talk about competition between us on the field over how many balls we might catch," said Brown, who had established his own All-Pro credentials since coming to the Raiders out of Notre Dame, where he won the Heisman Trophy as a senior in 1987.

"I knew better than that. Knowing Jerry as well as I did, I knew there would be no problem with that. We are good friends. But on the golf course, it's something entirely different."

Even though Rice and Brown both were avid golfers, they had never played a round together until the first of the Raiders' weekly games in 2001. Being pals, they decided they could share a golf cart for the game at Ruby Hill Golf Club in Livermore, a very challenging course designed by Jack Nicklaus.

Big mistake.

"They were riding in the cart and one of them was facing one way and the other was facing the exact opposite," said Shane Lechler, the Raiders' punter. "They wouldn't even talk to each other; they didn't want to look at each other. I mean, they were competitive that day. It was fun to watch them play."

Same as on the football field.

Tim Brown made the 1,000th reception of his career on Monday Night Football.

Jerry Rice catches a 48-yard touchdown pass in Super Bowl XXXVII.

Adam Treu replaced Robbins and played well enough, but Robbins is at least thirty pounds heavier, and the Raiders were unable to run the ball effectively without their best blocker.

Unable to step up in the pocket as he always has because nobody moves Robbins back, Gannon was sacked five times. After throwing ten interceptions all season, Gannon threw five in the Super Bowl—three were returned for touchdowns.

So which was the aberration, the first eighteen games or the Super Bowl? The Raiders have to think it was the latter.

Callahan wouldn't let it ruin his first season as a head coach.

"I take a lot of pride in what we have accomplished as a team," he said. "It was an incredible journey and to have played these last ten games; to go 9–1 in these last ten games, I thought was a real tribute leading up to the Super Bowl.

"We had been in playoff games for ten straight weeks coming into the Super Bowl. It was a tough journey and a journey that obviously . . . fell drastically short [in the Super Bowl], but we'll be a better team for that. All in all, this was a great season for us and the Oakland Raiders."

In their "Decades of Destiny," the Raiders have the best record in the NFL since Al Davis came to Oakland in 1963. They have played in Super Bowls in four of five decades. Oakland also had the best record, 33–15, in the first three years of the new century.

So the Raider Nation knows there is more to come.